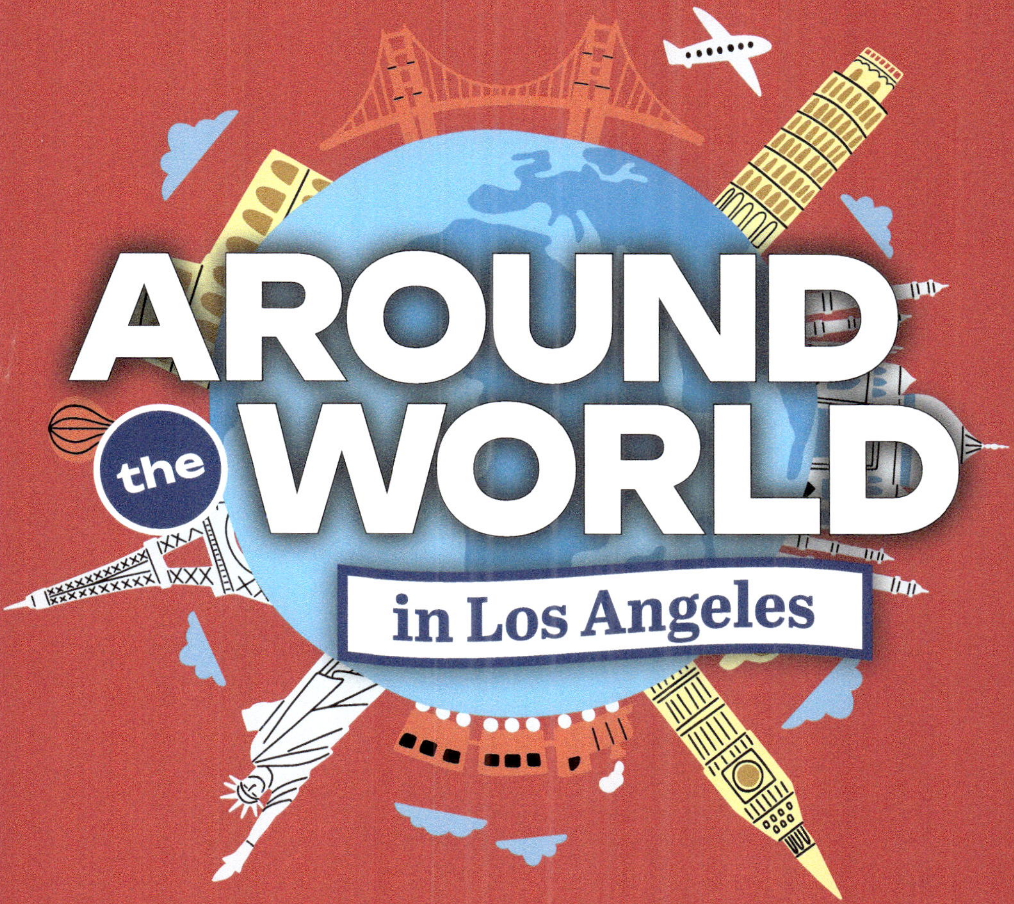

AROUND the WORLD in Los Angeles

Ruksana Hussain

REEDY PRESS

Reedy Press
PO Box 5131
St. Louis, MO 63139
reedypress.com

Library of Congress Control Number: 2024939005

ISBN: 9781681065441

Design: Richard Roden

Printed in Canada
24 25 26 27 28   5 4 3 2 1

Contents

Gallery At The Getty Center
Credit: Cassia Davis

Baar Baar LA interiors.
Credit: Regan Norton

Dedication

This book is dedicated to my family and friends, well-wishers, and acquaintances, who've encouraged me on my journey. And to Los Angeles, my home away from home.

Acknowledgments

Immense gratitude to Reedy Press, my colleagues in the writing and editing world, friends who cheered me on, my team, and everyone who has helped directly or indirectly in making this book a reality, especially all the community members who took the time to speak with me and the organizations and individuals contributing images.

Colombian appetizer at Selva. *Credit: Selva*

Festive spread at Bestia
Credit: Nicole Franzen

Introduction

Anyone who has ever called Los Angeles home will tell you the City of Angels is anything but heaven starting out. Finding your way in this monstrosity of a maze that stretches as far as it does wide isn't for the faint of heart. But it does make for a grand adventure as you experience communities, explore neighborhoods, and expand your horizons, whether it's cuisine or culture, arts or crafts, friends, or acquaintances. Every interaction leaves its impressions on the map of Los Angeles, veins and arteries connecting a throbbing city full of life and color and laughter and movement, all the time, everywhere. Let's experience all of that together.

One lifetime, one visit, one book can never encompass the vastness of the undertaking that is getting to know this city so I hope you will use this book to create your own map of adventures and find something in the process that maybe this book doesn't cover. Remember though that many venues and activities mentioned may not be available by the time you get around to it so please check ahead to ensure you are not disappointed. I hope to cross paths with you at some of these locations someday.

Santa Monica 3rd St Promenade. *Credit: City of Santa Monica*

Food And Celebrations

A One Afghan Market

Asian American and Pacific Islander Heritage Month in May

Chili Chutney Afghani restaurant

Eid and Ramadan celebrations

Family Halal Meat Market

Gleanoaks Kabab House

Halal Kitchen Café

Independence Day celebrations

Kausar Halal Meat Market

LA Chai Cart

Melad Bakery Restaurant and Catering

Naan Daagh Kabob Daagh restaurant

New Arrivals Supper Club

Nowroz Festival

Saffron Food Mart

Salar Nader music

Samia Karimi dance

Shor

Skewers Halal

World Refugee Day in June

Organizations And Institutions

Afghan American Community Organization

Afghanistan World Foundation

Afghans for a Better Tomorrow

Afghans Living in Los Angeles Facebook group

California Afghan DJ Services

Islamic Center of Southern California

Ketab Corporation Book Store

King Fahad Mosque

Masjid Bilal Islamic Center

Miry's List

Qabila Foundation

Southern California Cricket Association

The Norton Simon Museum South and Southeast Asian Painting and Sculpture Collection

West LA International Market

Afghan

The Afghan community in Los Angeles is a small but mighty group with representation primarily in the Northridge and Reseda areas within the county, with others calling Orange County home. Drive around those neighborhoods and you will find Afghan restaurants and markets within proximity to each other where you can experience their food and hospitality, no doubt.

LA Chai Cart's gourmet chai and biscuits cart. *Credit:Thanh Lai*

Afghan arts and music are more of a rare commodity with a show here and there to take advantage of. Los Angeles-based Negine Sekandari informs and amuses with her stand-up storytelling, artists like Shamsia Hassani express themselves through art and mural work, and dance performances by individual artists such as Samia Karimi are a treat to behold. While the community congregates to celebrate annual festivals such as Eid and Ramadan, access to cultural resources is more viable online with many organizations making Afghan music, literature, art, cinema, and other resources accessible to all.

SHOR in Hawaiian Gardens offers flavors inspired by Afghanistan, India, and Pakistan. *Credit: Andrew Bui*

African American/ Black

CAAM preserves the history, art, and culture of African Americans. *Credit: California African American Museum*

The annual African American Heritage Month celebration in Los Angeles in February is the best time to visit, celebrate, and support the Black community in the city. But that doesn't have to stop during the year and Black Owned in LA is a wealth of knowledge to turn to for activities year-round. Highly anticipated is the Destination Crenshaw project, a 1.3-mile stretch on Crenshaw Boulevard celebrating the city's Black legacy. This largest Black public art project in the country features works of more than 100 artists. Sankofa Park will be a public gathering space near here. Other points of interest include the Biddy Mason Memorial near Pershing Square Station, the Martin Luther King Jr. Memorial at Kenneth Hahn State Recreation Area, Obama Boulevard, the Grammy Museum, and more. Leimert Park has a self-guided art walk to explore galleries and historic buildings, and support area businesses. The Department of Cultural Affairs publishes an extensive guide of online and offline activities and venues to experience during the month pertaining to the annual theme. The California African American Museum in Exposition Park is one venue you shouldn't miss and especially during Heritage Month, the excellent programming here will have you returning soon.

Bohemian House of Espresso + Chai offers artisan chai. *Credit: Bohemian House*

Food And Celebrations

- African American Festival and Juneteenth at Aquarium of the Pacific
- African American Heritage Month
- African Restaurant Week
- Alta Adams Restaurant
- Blume and Plume Coffee
- Bohemian House of Espresso + Chai
- Champignon Eats
- Cuties Catering
- Harold and Belle's Creole
- NewFilmmakers Los Angeles Infocus: Black Cinema
- Pan African Film and Arts Festival
- Prosperity Market at the Natural History Museum
- Queen Squeeze Lemonade
- Rose Gold Pastries
- South LA Cafe
- The Gumbo Pot at the Farmers Market

Organizations And Institutions

- African American Cultural Center
- African American Firefighter Museum
- African Americans for LA Opera
- Art + Practice
- California African American Museum
- Ernie Wolfe Gallery
- Fowler Museum at UCLA Mellon African Art Initiative
- Inner City Cultural Center
- Kwanzaa Parade and Festival
- LA County Library Black Resource Center
- Los Angeles County Department of Parks and Recreation
- Lula Washington Dance Theater
- Malik Books
- Rele Art Gallery
- Reparations Club
- The National Association of African American Parents & Youth
- The William Grant Still Arts Center

Food And Celebrations

Alex Meat Market

Aquarium of the Pacific Noche de Estrellas

Bodega Malbec

Carlitos Gardel Argentine Steakhouse

Catalina's Market

Corrientes348 Argentinian Steakhouse

El Gaucho Meat Market

El Morfi Grill

Gaucho Beach Food Court

Gaucho Grill Argentine Steakhouse

Grand Casino Bakery and Cafe

Lala's Argentine Grill

Lord Empanada

Malbec Argentinian Cuisine

Mate Conmigo

Mercado Buenos Aires

Nonna's Empanadas

Pisco Sour Market

Qué Bárbaro

Rincon Argentino

The Chimi Grill

The Empanada Factory

Organizations And Institutions

Argentine Association

Heart of Samba Entertainment

International Society of Black Latinos

Museum of Latin American Art

Quitanda Family Market

Santiago Ceramica

Tango in LA Facebook group

Tango San Pedro

Tango Vibe shows and social dancing

The Broad

The Tango Room

Wara Andina

Wasi Clothing

Argentinian

Argentine architect Cesar Pelli left his mark on Los Angeles designing many important structures in the city including the Los Angeles International Airport Worldway Postal Center. One of his most recognizable works is the West Hollywood Pacific Design Center and the 777 Tower or the Pelli Tower in the Financial District. The red, green, and blue structures of the design center can be seen from miles away, turning it into a well-known landmark. Although open only to the design trade, there are chances to visit when private events are hosted. The prime location in West Hollywood cannot be denied. A short walk away and you are in the middle of boutiques, cars, hotels, and restaurants, usually very busy from office crowds, locals, and visitors finding a spot to people-watch. West Hollywood, or WeHo as locals call it, hosts many annual events including WeHo Pride LGBTQ Arts Festival and the Halloween Costume Carnaval. You'll find several Insta-worthy spots along here and if you are a reality-TV fan then you might even recognize some of the venues. Visit West Hollywood often shares tour ideas—the self-guided Golden Era Architecture tour is worth exploring.

Enjoy Tango classes and milongas at Tango San Pedro+Fiesta Latina.
Credit: Tango San Pedro

Lord Empanada's Nutella Banana Empanadas with Fudge Drizzle.
Credit: Lord Empanada

Armenian

The ultimate bite—Slices of Medovik (Russian Honey Cake) from Rose & Rye. *Credit: Rose and Kristine Jingozian and Rose & Rye Bakery*

Said to be the largest Armenian American population in the United States and the largest Armenian population outside of Armenia itself, LA's Armenian community mostly resides in East Hollywood, Glendale, Burbank, Pasadena, Montebello, and a few other neighborhoods but the designation of Little Armenia was bestowed upon part of East LA in 2000. You can get to Little Armenia via the LA Metro B Line. This area also has the Griffith Observatory for fabulous views of the city, and Barnsdall Art Park, which includes Frank Lloyd Wright's Hollyhock House, named to the UNESCO World Heritage List in 2019 and designated a Los Angeles Historic-Cultural Monument.

A highly anticipated event in the community is the opening of the Armenian American Museum and Cultural Center of California in 2025. Los Angeles is also home to several Armenian American celebrities including one of the most famous global music acts of all time, Cher (born Cherilyn Sarkisian), and professional tennis player Alexander Sarkissian. The probability of bumping into either is bleak. But the chances of dining at a Zankou Chicken, the popular chain of Armenian-owned restaurants with the original LA location at the corner of Sunset and Normandie, are extremely promising if you try.

Food And Celebrations

Ani Bakery

Armenian Film Festival

Armenian Genocide Remembrance / Memorial Day

Armenian History Month

Café Areni

Café Sheera

Carousel Restaurant

Esso Bistro

Falafel Arax

Flavors from Afar

Ginifest Armenian Wine and Spirits Festival

Koko's

Maggie's Pastry

Mantee Cafe

Marouch

Mechta International Deli

Mideast Tacos

Mini Kabob

Papillon Bakery

Rose & Rye Bakery

Sahags Basturma Sandwich Shop

Sarkis Pastry

Sasoun Bakery

Sasoun Produce

Taron Bakery

Tarzana Armenian Deli

The Armav

Venice Classic Pastry and Deli

Organizations And Institutions

Armenian Network of America Greater Los Angeles

GALAS LGBTQ+ Armenian Society

Gevorkian Dance Academy

Glendale Library Armenian History Month

Grand Park Genocide Memorial

Greek Armenian Association of Los Angeles

Hayastan Dance Center

Lark Musical Society Folk Instrument Ensemble

Montebello Genocide Memorial

Promise Armenian Institute UCLA

St. Garabed Armenian Apostolic Church

St. Gregory the Illuminator Cathedral

The Armenian Observer

Zvartnots Dance Ensemble

Food And Celebrations

Aussie Pies And Sausages

Australia Day celebrations in January

Belles Beach House

Bluestone Lane Coffee

Bronzed Aussie

Cobi's

Élephante

E.P. & L.P.

Grandmaster Recorders

Great White

Gum Tree Cafe and Shop

Gwen Butcher Shop & Restaurant

Little Ripper

Little Ruby's Cafe

Longshot Coffee

Maude

Melrose Rooftop Theatre

Merchant of Wine

Miss Melbourne Coffee

Red Window Coffee

Strings of Life

Tectonic Coffee

The Eveleigh

The Wine House

Wally's Wine

World Market

Organizations And Institutions

Australian Consulate-General in Los Angeles

Australian Garden at The Huntington

Australians in Film

Australians in Los Angeles Facebook group

Australian Music Alliance

Dragons Football Club

Eco Outdoor

Flannel

Gruin Gallery

Mark Whalen Studio

Paul Davies at Peter Mendenhall Gallery

Princess Polly

Ricky Swallow at David Kordansky Gallery

The Botanical Group

Toba Khedoori at Regen Projects

Wish You Were Here Group

Australian

Los Angeles is home to more Aussies than any other American city so there's a fair chance you might meet one at some point. Australia Day also provides the opportunity to indulge in Australian food and grand festivities marking the occasion. Chef Curtis Stone is a local culinary hero for his two dining establishments, Maude and Gwen Butcher Shop & Restaurant, which focus on celebrating Australian and Californian cuisine. For those visiting Los Angeles, dining at either Michelin-starred venue can be a once-in-a-lifetime experience. LA does have its fair share of Michelin-rated dining experiences if that guides your gastronomic choices. One way to score a great deal is to visit during one of two Dine Out Los Angeles editions every year when many highly rated restaurants present prix fixe menus. Several other Australian-owned coffee shops and restaurants provide an opportunity to indulge in pavlova, lamingtons, and meat pies. Many sought-after Australian clothing and lifestyle brands also have store locations in the area, and quite a few Australian-born or -based artists either call LA home or have their work displayed at city galleries. Grab yourself a flat white coffee and enjoy a great day of Aussie sightseeing.

At Gwen Butcher Shop & Restaurant, a pre-theater menu is available for guests. *Credit: Stan Lee*

Grandmaster Recorders has a rooftop, restaurant, and bar/lounge. *Credit: Jennifer Johnson*

Bangladeshi

Authentic, no-frills homemade biryani up for grabs from Little Bangladesh restaurants. *Credit: Ruksana Hussain*

In the grand scheme of things, Little Bangladesh is a recently designated neighborhood. It received official recognition in 2010 and then the city sign was installed in 2011. It is also one of the smallest in terms of area—a stretch along West 3rd Street across four blocks. Many Bangladeshi businesses share this space with other diverse-owned businesses but if you want to shop for South Asian groceries or enjoy as close to authentic, no-frills homemade cooking as you know homemade to be, then this is the exact four blocks within which you must tread.

Bangladeshi street-style snacks are some of the best solutions for a comfort food search. *Credit: Ruksana Hussain*

From snacks and chai to large dinner spreads and sugary treats to end with, the restaurants here are the last resort for many who need some comfort food to turn to. There are no major attractions or landmarks here as such. The attraction is in finding the right restaurant that will hit the home run on the taste test. The question is whether you are ready for that challenge.

Food And Celebrations

Al Noor

Al Watan

Aladin Sweets and Market

Amar Bangla

Asian American and Pacific Islander Heritage Month in May

Bangla Bazar and Restaurant

Bangladesh Mela

Biriyani Kabob House

Chargha House

Deshi Food and Groceries

Eid and Ramadan celebrations

Famous Tandoori

Halal Kabob House

Independence Day celebrations and parade

Kasturi Halal Meat and Grocery Store

Little Dhaka Restaurant and Grocery

Makkah Market

Royal Curry Café

Shahi Mahal

Spice Plus Restaurant and Grocery

Zam Zam Foods

Organizations And Institutions

Bangladesh Unity Federation of Los Angeles

Islamic Center of Southern California

King Fahad Mosque

Little Bangladesh

South Asian Network Bangladeshi Development Center

Southern California Cricket Association

The Norton Simon Museum South and Southeast Asian Painting and Sculpture Collection

West LA International Market

Food And Celebrations

Aroma Cafe

Belarus Freedom Day in March

EuroAsia Restaurant

European Deli Market

Kupala summer equinox holiday

Metro Cafe

Mom, Please Ukrainian Food

Now Serving

Oliv'e Food Market

Otto's European and Hungarian Import Store & Deli

Pacific Coast Food

Pierogi Cooking Class

Schreiner's Fine Sausages

Solidarity Restaurant

South East European Film Festival

Strada Eateria and Bar

Traktir

West LA International Market

World Refugee Day

Organizations And Institutions

Belarusian Freedom Mural

Belarusians in Los Angeles Instagram group

Kirk Douglas Theatre

Los Angeles County Museum of Art European Painting and Sculpture Collection

Sergio ArtG

UCLA exhibition research library

Wende Museum Belarusian Collection

Belarusian

The Belarusian community in Los Angeles came together in 2020 in response to the political scenario in their home country. Though Belarusians have lived in the city prior to then, this time the community came out in full force for a united cause. Since then, they have lobbied as a group and made their presence felt through community activism, cultural participation, and other avenues. As a much younger ethnic community, the members are dispersed but building a strong community.

Belarusian Freedom Mural.
Credit: Ruksana Hussain

Though there are several Hollywood celebrities with some Belarusian heritage such as Gwyneth Paltrow and Lisa Kudrow; they are generations removed. Among famous Belarusian celebrities globally are basketball player Yelena Leuchanka and tech entrepreneur Andrew Maximov. The most famous Belarusian known to Angelenos would be Kirk Douglas, born Issur Danielovitch, who passed away in 2020 at the age of 103. The Belarusian Jewish community in LA, even in Minsk, held memorial services to honor one of their most famous descendants. If you visit the Hollywood Walk of Fame, look for his star or go watch a show at the Kirk Douglas Theatre in Culver City. The theater is known for its adventurous new works and world premieres.

Belarusian: Handmade decorations in native Belarusian motifs made by Katya Ivanova. *Credit: Aliaksei Piatrovich*

Belizean

Spiritual drums displayed in one of three galleries at Garifuna Museum.
Credit: Media Marathon

Experiencing the Belizean community and culture in Los Angeles is easy. A search online will pull up multiple Belizean restaurants where you can have a meal featuring all the traditional dishes such as ducunu and panades (made with corn) and a variety of sumptuous stews. You can attend festivals and parades during the year that bring the community together and highlight their music, dance, and arts. The Garifuna Museum of Los Angeles—the first and only one of its kind in the United States—showcases the heritage and culture of the Garifuna people. Three galleries highlight collections of art and artifacts pertaining to everyday life, religion, and rituals.

Wanaragua warrior dancing with Euro mask at the Garifuna Museum.
Credit: Media Marathon

In 2001, UNESCO declared the language, dance, and music of the Garifuna an Intangible Cultural Heritage of Humanity that merits preserving. The museum seeks to collect all Garifuna-related materials to educate through exhibitions about art, music, dance, history, language, and heritage. Spots can be reserved online for a visit; tours are available daily but by appointment only.

Food And Celebrations

- Aquarium of the Pacific Noche de Estrellas
- Belize Fest
- Blue Hole Belizean Caribbean Cuisine
- Central American Festival and Parade
- Dat Moi Market
- El Katracho Honduran restaurant
- Garifuna International Indigenous Film Festival
- Garifuna Settlement Day Mass
- Joan and Sisters Belizean Creole Food
- La Bamba Fresh Island Cuisine
- Little Belize restaurant
- National Hispanic Heritage Month
- Now Serving
- Saraba Garifuna Cuisine
- The Pelican Belizean cuisine
- Tracey's Belizean restaurant

Organizations And Institutions

- Be Brave Beauty Supply
- Bilingual Foundation of the Arts
- Central American Confederation
- Consulate General of Belize
- Garifuna American Heritage Foundation United
- Garifuna Museum of LA
- Gracebank Creations Holistic Market
- Heart of Samba Entertainment
- Little Belize Community LA
- Museum of Latin American Art
- The Broad

Food And Celebrations

- Aquarium of the Pacific Noche de Estrellas
- Cabra restaurant
- Café Bolivar
- Dat Moi Market
- El Camaguey Meat Market
- El Morfi Grill
- Fogo de Chao
- Grand Casino Bakery and Cafe
- Greenfield Churrascaria
- HH Steakhouse
- Kravings Fusion Steakhouse and Lounge
- Llama Love Vegan
- Los Angeles Latino International Film Festival
- Los Balcones
- M Grill Steakhouse
- Nonna's Empanadas
- Pao's Pastries and Café
- Rosaline restaurant
- The Empanada Factory
- Valeu Espetos
- W Steakhouse

Organizations And Institutions

- American Bolivian Collective
- Bilingual Foundation of the Arts
- Consulate of Bolivia in Los Angeles
- Heart of Samba Entertainment
- International Society of Black Latinos
- Museum of Latin American Art
- Quitanda Family Market
- Santiago Ceramica
- The Broad
- Wara Andina
- Wasi Clothing

Bolivian

Most folks have a tough time pointing out Bolivia on a map or globe—the landlocked country is overshadowed by its larger, more famous neighbors like Brazil and Argentina. Even in Los Angeles, home to thousands from Bolivia, their South American neighbors continue to steal the spotlight. But if you chance upon a Bolivian celebration or restaurant here in LA, you will be pleasantly surprised by their food. Pao's Pastries and Café is one such location.

Saltenas filled with potato and protein are a popular Bolivian pastry snack. *Credit: Ruksana Hussain*

Los Angeles Bolivians will know teacher Jaime Escalante, whose name was etched in history for his efforts to teach upper-level math in the high-school education system of East LA and the film *Stand and Deliver*, which documented his struggles. Escalante was also featured on a United States Postal Service stamp, possibly the only Bolivian with that honor. In Hollywood, comic Martin Amini (unrelated to Max Amini, an Iranian American comic) and actress Raquel Welch are among the famous names some might recognize from the Bolivian community.

Dulce de leche cookie sandwiches called alfajores from Pao's Pastries and Café, possibly the only Bolivian restaurant in the metro LA area. *Credit: Ruksana Hussain*

Brazilian

Viver Brasil honors Brazil's African legacy through contemporary dance theater. *Credit: Elizabeth Asher*

Most Brazilian Americans reside in the Palms and Culver City areas. Culver City houses several capoeira schools but also is the place to go to support Brazilian businesses and events. If you've never tried capoeira, the martial art with rhythmic dance and acrobatic movements, here's your chance. Samba dance studios, on the other hand, aren't as common but you can still find a few to test your musicality.

If neither appeals to you, then learning to fashion a caipirinha at a mixology class somewhere in the vicinity is an option. Or better yet, just sign up for dinner and a live performance at Herb Alpert's Vibrato Jazz Grill where Brazilian singer, pianist, and composer Catina Deluna will entertain while you try a caipirinha concocted by your friendly bartender. For more of an outdoorsy experience, ArteSabor, the Brazilian cross-cultural food and art festival presents music, dance, food, and entertainment galore. If you enjoy that, then plan to attend the annual Carnaval party for an even more elaborate celebration.

Capoeira practitioners playing at Brasil Brasil Cultural Center. *Credit: Brasil Brasil Cultural Center*

Food And Celebrations

30 South Brazilian Fast Food

Aquarium of the Pacific Noche de Estrellas

Bossa Nova

Brazilian Plate House

Café Brasil

Caipirinha Bar

Carnaval party

El Camaguey Meat Market

Fogo de Chao

Greenfield Churrascaria

HH Steakhouse

Kravings Fusion Steakhouse and Lounge

La Vaca Grill

M Grill Steakhouse

Maya's Brigadeiro Brazilian Sweets

Pampas Grill Churrascaria

Panelas

Pisco Sour Market

Schreiner's Fine Sausages

Señoreata

Tapizon Brazilian Asian Fusion

Ubatuba Acai

Valeu Espetos

W Steakhouse

Organizations And Institutions

Brasil Brasil Cultural Center

Brazil California Chamber of Commerce

Brazilian Nites Productions

CaliSamba

Capoeira Besouro

Capoeira Brasil

Capoeira DTLA

Consulate General of Brazil

Heart of Samba Entertainment

Hi Brazil Market

International Samba Congress

International Society of Black Latinos

Los Angeles Brazilian Film Festival

Museum of Latin American Art

Quitanda Family Market

Rio Brasil Entertainment

Supermercado Brazil

The Broad

Viver Brasil Dance Company

Food And Celebrations

Britannia Pub

BritWeek

Hotel Bel-Air Afternoon Tea

Kings Row Gastropub

Little John's Candies at The Original Farmer's Market

London's Pub & Grill

Los Angeles Biltmore Rendezvous Court Café Afternoon Tea

Lucky Baldwin's

Pickwick's Pub

Robin Hood British Pub

Santa Monica Proper Afternoon Tea

The Cat and Fiddle

The Fox and Hounds

The Stalking Horse Brewery & Freehouse

The Wizarding World of Harry Potter at Universal Studios Hollywood

White Harte Pub

Ye Olde King's Head

Organizations And Institutions

British American Business Council

British and European Art Collection at The Huntington

British Consulate-General in Los Angeles

Brits in LA Facebook group

BWI Imports

Independent Shakespeare Company

Los Angeles County Museum of Art European Painting and Sculpture Collection

Southern California Cricket Association

The British Connection

The British Weekly

The Mayflower Club

The Queen Mary

Theodore Payne Foundation for Wildflowers & Native Plants

British

Santa Monica is sometimes referred to as Little Britain given the number of English pubs within a short radius just minutes from the ocean. Many annual events are offered here—British and otherwise—which include Taste of Main Street, Beach Sports Summer Festival, Americana at the Park, and ice skating at the downtown Santa Monica rink in winter. Walk out onto the pier, which has its own amusement park and the world's only solar-powered Ferris wheel and roller coaster. For avid Anglophiles, afternoon teas can be enjoyed at area hotels such as the Fairmont Miramar and The Georgian, as well as The Biltmore Los Angeles, The Peninsula Beverly Hills, The London West Hollywood, The Culver Hotel, the Rose and Blanc Tearoom, Valerie Confections, and several other venues in Los Angeles. When it comes to British influences beyond beers and teas, you will notice some fine examples of 1920s-style storybook house architecture at Spadena House, Hobbit House, Charlie Chaplin cottages and studios, and Snow White cottages—can't miss that fairytale-cottage look as you pass by these striking structures. Victorian homes in a variety of styles are also found in Los Angeles albeit mainly in historic neighborhoods like West Adams and Angelino Heights.

Afternoon Tea at The Biltmore amid its splendid architecture and historic interiors.
Credit: The Biltmore Los Angeles

A little British pub experience at The Cat and Fiddle.
Credit: Oscar Jimenez

Bulgarian

XoroTroptzi dance ensemble performing at a Consulate of Republic of Bulgaria reception. *Credit: Victoria Sirakova*

Though a small community in Los Angeles, Bulgarians have a cultural organization, the Bulgarian Education and Culture Society, serving both Los Angeles and Orange counties, that hosts events such as community socials and cultural performances. Follow the group online for information on upcoming Bulgarian cultural experiences. The dance troupe XoroTroptzi was formed through the cultural organization, initially to share traditional dances among friends, but went on to become the only Bulgarian folk ensemble in the city. Now the group performs for the community and at heritage festivals across the United States and Canada. Los Angeles hosts only a few performances annually so you may need to consult the troupe's website for dates and locations of future performances.

Hollywood actor Jon Voight is of Bulgarian descent and received a Special Award of Consul of Bulgaria in the USA in 2023, given occasionally in recognition of those who have filmed in Bulgaria or are connected to Bulgarian culture. Bulgaria is considered among the best destinations in Europe for film production thanks to its infrastructure, unique locations, and other film commission benefits. Many Hollywood and international movies have filmed in the capital, Sofia, and other parts of Bulgaria.

Food And Celebrations

- Antoanela's Bakery
- Aroma Cafe
- Black Jack Market
- Divino
- European Deli Market
- Kiff Kafe
- Lemon Poppy
- Mechta International Deli
- Metro Cafe
- Mignon Wine Bar
- Monta Factory
- Now Serving
- Otto's European and Hungarian Import Store & Deli
- Pacific Coast Food Posto896
- San Pedro Cafe
- Schreiner's Fine Sausages
- Sebastian's Mediterranean
- South East European Film Festival
- Strada Eateria and Bar
- Sunset Grill Hollywood
- Sweets A LA-Cluj
- Traktir
- West LA International Market

Organizations And Institutions

- Blind Lizard Balkan Band
- Bulgarian American Cultural Educational Society of California
- Bulgarian Eastern Orthodox Church-St. George
- Bulgarian Education and Culture Society
- Bulgarians in Los Angeles Facebook group
- Consulate General of Bulgaria in Los Angeles
- Los Angeles County Museum of Art European Painting and Sculpture Collection
- Nevenka Folk Ensemble
- XoroTroptzi Dance Ensemble

Food And Celebrations

Annual Myanmar New Year/Water Festival

Asia Supermarket

Asian American and Pacific Islander Heritage Month in May

Bagan Burmese Kitchen

Burmese Please

Jasmine Market and Deli

Kim Thai Food

Los Angeles Asian Film Festival

Los Angeles Asian Pacific Film festival

Mandalay's Morning Star

Mutiara Halal Food and Market

Now Serving

Owl Owl Thai Lao Street Food

Rangoon California Burmese Food House

Sabaidee Lao & Thai Street Food

Southeast Asia Day at the Aquarium of the Pacific

Yoma Myanmar

Organizations And Institutions

LA Myanmar Christian Church

Los Angeles Burmese Community

Los Angeles City Myanmar society

Los Angeles County Museum of Art South and Southeast Asian Art Collection

Myanmar Consulate-General, Los Angeles

Network of Myanmar American Association

UCLA Center for Southeast Asian Studies

Burmese

The New Year celebration of Thingyan and the Film Festival in Los Angeles are the best ways to experience the Burmese community and participate in their annual celebrations of culture and the arts. Despite the fact that the Burmese have no ethnic enclave in LA à la Thai Town or Koreatown, the city has many Burmese dining venues. They all have delicious offerings such as mohinga, a rice noodle and fish soup, and tea-leaf salad, featuring fermented tea leaves. Burmese cuisine is one of only a handful of cuisines where tea leaves are eaten.

Mohinga or fish chowder noodle soup is a must at a Burmese restaurant. *Credit: Ruksana Hussain*

Make it a point to experience this charming culture through an event and/or by trying Burmese food. Follow up your mohinga with a traditional Burmese dessert like jaggery—the Burmese version of chocolate which may come either as a ball or on a stick, and semolina cake, which is baked with semolina flour and coconut milk, and found in a variety of shapes and colors. All are noticeably different from other Asian desserts you may have tried.

Try a traditional Burmese tea leaf salad at area restaurants. *Credit: Ruksana Hussain*

Cambodian

Cambodia Town Parade and Culture Festival's dance performances.
Credit: Cambodiatown

Make your way down the coast to Long Beach to visit the area officially designated as Cambodia Town in 2007. Several Cambodian businesses are here but most important, the annual Cambodia Town Parade and Culture Festival occurs here as well. A full day of festivities featuring dance, music, food, arts, and other programming will draw you in to celebrate with the community. At the Long Beach Khmer Kickboxing Center, you can learn more about the ancient Cambodian martial art Khun Khmer or Bokator or attend a Cambodian classical dance performance or workshop by Modern Apsara Company. Cambodian Restaurant Week, Film Festival, and Heritage Month celebrations are also hosted here. If you'd like to try some fish amok (steamed fish in banana leaf) or kralan (dessert made with rice) then you are in for a treat as several area restaurants have that and more on the menu. Watch out for colorful murals by local artist Sayon Syprasoeuth, also known for his widely exhibited paintings, public art, and sculptures. He is also one of eight artists involved in the Cambodia Town Mural Project featuring a collection of eight public art murals along the Cambodia Town business corridor.

Community members participate in a ritual ahead of the Cambodia Town Parade and Culture Festival celebrations.
Credit: Cambodiatown

Food And Celebrations

- A&J Seafood Shack
- Battambong BBQ
- Cambodia Town Film Festival
- Cambodian Heritage Month celebrations in April
- Golden Lake Eatery
- Hak Heang Restaurant
- Khmer Town Chinese Food & BBQ
- Koh Ruessei (Bamboo Island) Noodles
- Mama Twako
- Naga Café Khmer Street Food
- Phnom Penh Noodle Shack
- Pho Hong Phat
- RiceString Noodle Shack
- Sankranta New Year celebrations
- Shlap Muan I 1st Khmer Chicken Wings
- Sophy's: Cambodia Town Food & Music
- The Golden Skewer Cambodian Street Food

Organizations And Institutions

- Arts Council for Long Beach
- Cambodia Town Mural Project
- Historical Society of Long Beach
- Long Beach Cambodian Restaurant Week
- Los Angeles County Library Asian Pacific Resource Center
- Los Angeles County Museum of Art South and Southeast Asian Art Collection
- TeAda Productions
- The Norton Simon Museum South and Southeast Asian Painting and Sculpture
- United Cambodian Community
- USC Asian Museum
- USC Fisher Museum of Art

Food And Celebrations

- Alex Meat Market
- Aquarium of the Pacific Noche de Estrellas
- Cabra restaurant
- Catalina's Market
- Chilean Fest
- Chilenazo restaurant
- Dat Moi Market
- El Camaguey Meat Market
- El Morfi Grill
- Grand Casino Bakery and Cafe
- Llama Love Vegan
- Lord Empanada
- Los Angeles Latino International Film Festival
- Los Balcones
- Nonna's Empanadas
- Now Serving
- Pampas Grill Churrascaria
- Rincon Chileno restaurant
- Rosaline restaurant
- The Empanada Factory
- Valeu Espetos
- W Steakhouse

Organizations And Institutions

- Bilingual Foundation of the Arts
- Chile America California Foundation
- Heart of Samba Entertainment
- International Society of Black Latinos
- Museum of Latin American Art
- Quitanda Family Market
- Santiago Ceramica
- The Broad
- Wara Andina
- Wasi Clothing

Chilean

Los Angeles may have other connections to Chile, but most people can usually suggest two—actor Pedro Pascal and a pisco sour. It is unlikely that you will encounter Pascal in a visit to the city but you are almost guaranteed a good pisco sour at one of the restaurants listed here. A popular cocktail in Peru, a good local version of the pisco sour in Los Angeles can be found at Lock&Key, Baltaire, or the Normandie Club.

Chimichurri on asada option from Lord Empanada.
Credit: Lord Empanada

Even better, plan your trip to include one of the many cocktail festivals here in the City of Angels. The Los Angeles Cocktail Class would be one way to accomplish that. But if you miss those dates, LA is full of innovative mixologists who can craft unique and delicious cocktails for you. Plan for at least one meal at Rincon Chileno—the East Hollywood restaurant celebrated 50 years of serving Los Angeles with Chilean delicacies such as empanadas and tortas in 2023. Not only is this a spot for visitors to try but one that the local Chilean American community swears by. Estofado (beef stew) and pastel de choclo (baked corn casserole) are among the crowd favorites from the menu.

Lord Empanada's cocktail-size empanadas for special events.
Credit: Lord Empanada

Chinese

The Formosa first opened its doors in Hollywood in 1939. *Credit: 1933 Group*

First stop: Chinatown. Although this is a good starting point for experiencing Chinese culture in Los Angeles, the San Gabriel Valley and other parts of the county have larger Chinese populations overall. The Undiscovered Chinatown tour is one way to immerse yourself in all things Chinese American. The other is a free self-guided walking tour using the handy map by Angels Walk (they have guides for other neighborhoods, too). The Los Angeles Conservancy has a self-guided tour booklet as well. If you arrive in Chinatown by Metro, the train station here has a pagoda theme. Another well-known landmark designed to resemble a pagoda is Grauman's Chinese Theatre—sign up for the theater tour and watch a movie on IMAX while you are here. Many films were shot in Chinatown including global superstar Jackie Chan's *Rush Hour*. The restaurant Foo Chow has its claim to fame announced on the exterior wall—you simply cannot miss it. Bruce Lee fans can find his 7-foot-tall bronze statue in the Central Plaza. Look for the gateway monuments on the east and west ends of Chinatown or stop in at Thien Hau Temple's impressive structure in red and gold.

The Institute for Art and Olfaction is a nonprofit organization in Chinatown. *Credit: The Institute for Art and Olfaction*

Food And Celebrations

- Asian American and Pacific Islander Heritage Month in May
- Bobafest
- Chifa Chinese Peruvian
- China Café at Grand Central Market
- China Depot at The Original Farmers Market
- Chinatown Moon Festival
- Chinese Film Festival
- Firecracker Run/Walk
- Hui Tou Xiang
- Ixlb Dimsum
- Lunar New Year Celebration
- Mao's Kitchen
- Mian Taste Sichuan Noodle
- Miss LA Chinatown Pageant
- Phoenix Inn
- Sichuan Impression
- Springfest
- Steep LA Tea Room
- Tasty Noodle House Shanghai Cuisine
- The Formosa
- Yang Chow Mandarin & Szechuan Cuisine

Organizations And Institutions

- Charlie James Gallery
- Chinatown Business Improvement District
- Chinatown Central Plaza
- Chinatown Metro Station
- Chinese American Museum
- Chinese Chamber of Commerce
- Chinese Culture Development Center
- Chinese Historical Society
- Coagula
- First Chinese Baptist Church
- Institute for Art and Olfaction
- LA County Library Asian Pacific Resource Center
- LeBasse Projects
- Los Angeles County Museum of Art Chinese Art Collection
- The Norton Simon Museum South and Southeast Asian Sculpture collection
- Thien Hau Temple

Food And Celebrations

African Obichi Food Store

Afro-Latinx Festival

Aquarium of the Pacific Noche de Estrellas

Arepas Caseras Colombianas

Colombian Delicatessen

Dat Moi Market

El Festival Colombiano

El Molinito

El Paisa

La Casa De Las Parilladas

La Chiva Colombian Lonchera

La Fonda Antioqueña

La Maria

Macondo Kitchen

National Hispanic Heritage Month

Pisco Sour Market

Sabor Colombiano

Sazon Colombia

Selva

Sus Arepas

Tropic Ice Dessert Shop

Vivi's Gourmet Cuisine

WezzArepas

Organizations And Institutions

Avenue 50 Studio

Bermudez Projects

Bilingual Foundation of the Arts

Consulate of Colombia in Los Angeles

La Diosa

La Galeria Rebelde

La Placita Church

La Plaza de Cultura y Artes

Latino Outdoors

Latino Theater Company

Museum of Latin American Art

The Broad

The Granada

The Mistake Room

Vincent Price Art Museum

Colombian

Grab some arepas—meat or cheese-filled hand pies—and a flavorful bold Colombian coffee at any Los Angeles coffee shop or roaster to enjoy a sunny day in the city. And what better way to do it than with CicLAvia, when Los Angeles streets are closed to car traffic and turn into free public spaces with access for all to walk, bike, skate, and tour supporting area businesses and local communities in the process? The neighborhoods and routes change often so check online before you go. CicLAvia is, in fact, inspired by the ciclovias held in Bogota, Colombia, on Sundays. Food festivals, food halls, and food trucks are common in Los Angeles, and you are guaranteed to find a few spots to grab some delicious empanadas, which are sweet and savory pastries, or ajiaco, a filling chicken and potato soup. But before you call it a day, check to see if there is a festival celebration or a musical act at one of the city's coveted performance venues where you can experience some cumbia music or salsa dancing.

WezzArepas offers Arepa de Choclo, sweet cornbread with mozzarella cheese. *Credit WezzArepas.*

Arroz Chaufa at Selva, a Colombian-inspired restaurant, helmed by Cali native Chef Carlos Jurado. *Credit: Selva*

Costa Rican / Panamanian

Caribbean Soul Kitchen's Panamanian delicacies include Carimanola yuca balls. *Credit: Caribbean Soul Kitchen*

Folks in Los Angeles love their coffee, especially when brewed at a neighborhood coffee shop. Even better if the café offers coffees from other parts of the world. Costa Rican coffee is served in many local shops, but Calle Lajas from Lamill Silver Lake will send you on a journey to learn more about the land of exceptional coffee beans. There's a lot of information online about coffee shops to explore in the city, and depending on your preferences, you are sure to find one you'd like to spend a few minutes or hours at.

Some coffee shops to add to your list as you wander around Los Angeles are 10 Speed Coffee in Calabasas, Laidrey Coffee Roasters in Tarzana, Cognoscenti Coffee Roasters in Culver City, and Patria Coffee Roasters in Compton. However, the Los Angeles Coffee Festival is a must for any coffee lovers working on finding the right flavor to start their mornings on the right note. But if you don't make it to the festival then no worries—the folks at Café de Leche or Calabasas Coffee Co. can also make you a flavorful cup of Costa Rican coffee to savor on your jaunt around town.

Food And Celebrations

- Aquarium of the Pacific Noche de Estrellas
- Café de Leche
- Café Integral at Freehand Hotel
- Calabasas Coffee Co.
- Caribbean American Heritage Month celebrations in June
- Caribbean Soul Kitchen
- Central American Festival and Parade
- Dat Moi Market
- Films from Panama and the Americas Festival
- Museum of Latin American Art Afro-Latinx Festival
- National Hispanic Heritage Month
- Ora's Kitchen
- Panamanian Independence Day
- Picaresca Barra De Cafe & Casa Tostadora
- Portobanco's restaurant
- Reyes Coffee
- Si Mon

Organizations And Institutions

- Ballet Folklorico
- Bilingual Foundation of the Arts
- Central American Confederation
- Consulate of Panama in California
- Craft Contemporary
- Heart of Samba Entertainment
- Institute of Contemporary Art
- Los Angeles County Museum of Art
- Museum of African American Art
- Museum of Latin American Art
- The Broad
- Translatina Coalition
- Viva Panama

Food And Celebrations

A-1 Imported Groceries Italian Market & Deli

Aroma Cafe

Black Jack Market

CHA CHA Cuterie Board

Croatian Culture Week

Croatian Wine Tasting & Dinner

Divino

Kiff Kafe

Los Angeles Football Club Croatian Heritage Night

Mignon Wine Bar

Monta Factory

Now Serving

Pirozzi's Italian Deli

San Pedro Cafe

San Pedro Film Festival

Sebastian's Mediterranean

South East European Film Festival

South Shores Meat San Pedro

Southern California Croatian Bocce Ball Tournament

Organizations And Institutions

Consulate General of the Republic of Croatia

Croatian American Club

Croatian American Hall of San Pedro

Croatian National Association and Foundation

Los Angeles Public Library International Languages Department

Los Angeles Vatreni Community

SC Croat San Pedro

St. Anthony Croatian Catholic Church

Croatian

The Croatian American Hall in Croatia Place in San Pedro. *Credit: Ruksana Hussain*

As you drive through San Pedro, you'll know immediately when you are in Croatian Place. On one end is the Cultural Center and on the other is the Croatian Club. The Croatian presence here has grown over the years to the point where the inaugural Croatian Culture Week occurred in 2023 and included several events that were open to the local Croatian community and the general public.

Past community celebrations have included live music and dancing, home-cooked traditional delicacies such as lamb and mostaccoli (a pasta dish) and performances of the Croatian folk dance, kolo. The first Croatian Heritage Night was also hosted by the Los Angeles Football Club, which has been hosting similar heritage nights for other cultures and communities for years now. If in San Pedro, visit some of their annual events. A Polar Bear New Year Swim, Whale Festival, Grand Grunion Gala, Shakespeare by the Sea, and Holiday Boat Ride and Parade are just some of the fun festivities in store.

Cuban

Porto's Northridge Bakery showcase of cakes. *Credit: Porto's Bakery and Café*

The Cuban community has a strong presence in Los Angeles, as evidenced by the plethora of cafés, restaurants, festivals, or examples of Cuban arts. But if you are in or visiting Los Angeles and do not experience the iconic Porto's Bakery and Café, then you've missed out. They make it easy for you, too, with multiple locations across the county and the option to order online. But part of the experience is waiting in line before the doors open (yes, there is always a line—it's an institution!) and finally making it to the display case to choose from their mouth-watering selection of pastries. Some folks may be partial to their guava and cheese strudels or the tres-leches cakes, but you will learn that each visit brings many more options. Don't worry though; Porto's Bakery and Café isn't going anywhere—the family-owned business has been around for generations so it's a good bet that they'll still be there to welcome you when you go back for more. But if you simply can't get enough, then grab some of their Bake-at-Home options and now you can enjoy Porto's at home too.

Porto's signature Mango Mousse Bomb is a crowd favorite. *Credit: Porto's Bakery and Café*

Food And Celebrations

Aquarium of the Pacific Noche de Estrellas

Baracoa Cuban Café

Café Cuba and Cakes

Caribbean American Heritage Month celebrations in June

Caribbean Music and Arts Festival

Coco Palm

Cuban American Music Festival

El Floridita

El Mambi Market

El Nuevo Mundo Market

Gigi's Café Cubano

Havana Mania

La Cubana

Long Beach Reggae Festival

Made in Havana

Mamey Miami

Mercedes Bar and Grille

My Havana Vieja

National Hispanic Heritage Month

Porto's Bakery and Café

Soto's Cuban Kitchen

Taste of Carnaval Hollywood

Tropicana Bakery and Cuban Café

Versailles Comida Cubana

Organizations And Institutions

Avenue 50 Studio

Bermudez Projects

Bilingual Foundation of the Arts

Caribbean American & Heritage Foundation, Inc.

Cuban Heritage Los Angeles

Dat Moi Market

Heart of Samba Entertainment

Hispanics for Los Angeles Opera

La Diosa

La Galeria Rebelde

La Placita Church

La Plaza de Cultura y Artes

Latino Outdoors

Latino Theater Company

Museum of Latin American Art

Pico Rivera Sports Arena

The Broad

The Granada

The Mistake Room

Food And Celebrations

Ava Krō

Berolina Bakery

Bulle Bakery

Clark Street Bread

Constitution Day

Copenhagen Pastry

ilcaffè los angeles

Kustaa Cheese and Wine

Midsummer celebrations

Nordic Oscars Week celebrations

Nordic Spirit Symposium

Open Face Food Shop

Scandinavian Festival

Scandinavian Film Festival

Scandinavian Kitchen in LA

Schreiner's Fine Sausages

Shoop's European Market and Café

So Cal Scandinavian Dancing

Sockerbit Swedish Candy Shop

The Magic Nut and Candy Co.

Viking Pizza and Kabob

Organizations And Institutions

& other stories clothing store

Acne Studios clothing

Anine Bing fashion

COS clothing

Danish Modern North Hollywood

Danish National Committee of Southern California

Denmark 50

Duxiana Furniture store

European Languages and Movies in America

Fjällräven North America

Happy Socks

Hästens Beds

Hostler Burrows design gallery

Huset shop

Ikea

Los Angeles Public Library International Languages Department

Malibu Farm Restaurant and Café

Nordic Spirit Classics Second Friday Series

Nudie Jeans Co

Royal Danish Consulate

Scandinavian American Cultural Center and Historical Foundation

Scandinavian Designs Furniture

Danish

For a taste of Scandinavian candy, shop at Sockerbit. *Credit: Sockerbit*

While the Danish American Club, the Danish Church and Cultural Center, and a few other points of interest are in Orange County, Los Angeles has a few spots to visit as well, including Copenhagen Bakery—your destination for Danish pastries such as kringle, rumkugle, and kransecake. A few other cultural events through the year provide opportunities to indulge in the festivities this Scandinavian community brings to LA, but most Angelenos will tell you the best place to experience all things Danish would be in Solvang, considered the Danish Capital of America, which is a 2.5-hour drive north. Aebleskiver (pancake balls), rye bread, waffles, and frikadeller (meatballs), among other Danish delicacies, are your reward for making the journey over. The downtown area hosts the annual Julefest, which is a monthlong holiday celebration, and Solvang Danish Days, a three-day heritage festival. As with most celebrations as these, expect to reserve your stay and other local sightseeing in advance—the quick drive over sees many Angelenos escaping for the weekend as well. If staying in LA, then the Scandinavian film festival is a fun way to spend the day. For the latest events in the Scandinavian community, visit A Viking in LA online.

Dominican

The Dominicans by Chef Cruze's precast frito (fried fish). *Credit: The Dominicans*

A few years ago, Los Angeles had absolutely no Dominican offerings in its culinary showcase—a point of frustration for visitors and residents, considering a few thousands of the community are LA residents. However, the city now boasts a growing number of Dominican restaurants that represent this vibrant culture and community. Venues serving pernil and maduros—roasted pork shoulder and sweet, fried plantains, respectively—and other traditional dishes are popping up around the city, which is welcoming them into its already brimming restaurant scene.

Hat tip to the new entrants to the LA food scene for giving the city that opportunity. The eateries are scattered all over Los Angeles so plan your transportation and dining experiences accordingly. Positively stop by El Bacano in North Hollywood for your fill of bacalao guisado (salted codfish in tomato sauce), sancocho Dominicano (three-meat strew) and a handful of other house favorites lovingly prepared by the Santana family. Makes for a fun break in your day sightseeing through the North Hollywood Arts District area.

The Dominicans by Chef Cruze's chicken and cheese empanadas. *Credit: The Dominicans*

Food And Celebrations

African Obichi Food Store

Afro-Latino Culture Fest

Afro-Latinx Festival

Aquarium of the Pacific Noche de Estrellas

Carnaval celebrations

Dat Moi Market

El Bacano

El Coro Café

El Diamante

El Mambi Market

El Molinito

Independence celebrations in February

Karibbean Cuisine Los Angeles

La Maria

National Hispanic Heritage Month

Now Serving

Selva

Sus Arepas

The Dominicans Kitchen

Tropic Ice Dessert Shop

Vivi's Gourmet Cuisine

WezzArepas

Organizations And Institutions

Avenue 50 Studio

Bermudez Projects

Bilingual Foundation of the Arts

Consulate General of Dominican Republic in Los Angeles

La Diosa

La Galeria Rebelde

La Placita Church

La Plaza de Cultura y Artes

Latino Outdoors

Latino Theater Company

Museum of Latin American Art

The Broad

The Granada

The Mistake Room

Translatina Coalition

Food And Celebrations

Cooking with Keasberry

Dutch American Heritage Day celebration in November

Holland Festival in May

Holland International Market

Indo Bistro

King's Day celebrations (Koningsdag) in April

LaaLaaPan

Medan Kitchen

Mee and Greet

Merry's House of Chicken

Mr. Sate restaurant

Noodle Stars

Oma's Puffers

Plus62 Street Food

Satay Indonesian Delights

Shoop's European Deli and Café

Simpang Asia Restaurant

Stop Bye Café Indonesian Fusion Food Truck

Sweet Amsterdam Food Truck

Tip Top Mart

Wallflower

Organizations And Institutions

Getty Center

Los Angeles County Museum of Art European Painting and Sculpture Collection

Los Angeles Public Library International Languages Department

Netherlands Business Support Office Los Angeles

The Netherland America Foundation (NAF) SoCal Chapter

The Norton Simon Museum

Dutch

Every April, the Dutch and Dutch-Indonesian community meet to celebrate King's Day in Long Beach. The annual occasion attracts almost 2,000 visitors, including community members from other states. The Dutch Indonesians are descendants of those who migrated from the former Dutch East Indies, now Indonesia, so they have a blend of both Dutch and Indonesian influences in their culture.

The Holland Festival is an Amsterdam-style springtime outdoor party.
Credit: Jeff Keasberry

Jeff Keasberry is a Los Angeles chef and author who has been working to preserve the Dutch-Indonesian culture and raise awareness of it in the United States, sharing Dutch and Indonesian food and cooking techniques through events and classes. While options for Dutch and Dutch-Indo dining are few, Indonesian restaurants are many in the Los Angeles area and several participate in the annual event. If the enticing aroma of food doesn't announce the event, the sea of orange certainly will. Orange is the color of the Dutch royal family, so the community takes advantage of any occasion to don it. Dutch American Heritage Day (November 16) is another occassion when the Dutch and Dutch-Indo community congregates for celebrations.

Ecuadorian

Ecuadorian papas con cuero from Dulcisfama. *Credit: Dulcisfama*

Los Angeles loves a good parade; just announce one and watch the fun! The Ecuadorian community organizes a parade and a festival, attracting large crowds. The Taste of Ecuador is one of the largest cultural community events in the city. People are excited to participate and food vendors selling ceviche (marinated seafood) and asado (South American barbecue) only sweeten the deal. And, of course, there are always several other parties organized by local businesses and community members associated with it, so make plans for that too. If you tried charting out all the parades in LA, you'd see that there's one almost every week.

Parade season begins with the Rose Bowl Parade in January and ends with holiday parades in December. In between, you will find everything from Golden Dragon and St. Patrick's Day parades to Memorial and Labor Day parades as well. So go ahead—bring your parade-loving self to one or two of these events, and enjoy the camaraderie.

Dulcisfama's Tigrillo is a popular breakfast dish. *Credit: Dulcisfama*

Food And Celebrations

- Aquarium of the Pacific Noche de Estrellas
- Catalina's Market
- Dat Moi Market
- Dulcisfama Bakery
- Ecuador Independence Day Parade and Festival
- El Molinito
- El Paisa
- La Casa De Las Parilladas
- La Fonda Antioqueña
- Las Guayacas Qué Chévere
- Los Angeles Latino International Film Festival
- Manjares de mi Tierra
- National Hispanic Heritage Month
- Selva
- Sus Arepas
- Taste of Ecuador Food Festival
- Tropic Ice Dessert Shop
- Vivi's Gourmet Cuisine
- WezzArepas

Organizations And Institutions

- Avenue 50 studio
- Bilingual Foundation of the Arts
- Consulate of Ecuador
- La Galeria Rebelde
- La Placita Church
- La Plaza de Cultura y Artes
- LaPau Gallery
- Latino Outdoors
- Latino Theater Company
- Los Angeles County Museum of Art's Art of the Ancient Americas and Latin American Contemporary Art Collection
- Museum of Latin American Art
- Plaza Park
- The Broad
- The Floricanto Center for the Performing Arts
- The Mistake Room
- Translatina Coalition

Food And Celebrations

- Al Layali Restaurant & Café
- Anwar's Kitchen
- Arab American Heritage Month celebrations in April
- Aunt Yvette's Kitchen
- Bavel
- Bowery Bungalow
- Carousel Restaurant
- Dune Mediterranean
- FurnSaj Bakery & Restaurant
- Joe's Falafel
- King's Kabob
- Kismet
- Malek's Grill and Kabob
- Mini Kabob
- Mizlala Mediterranean
- Open Sesame Grill
- Pan African Film and Arts Festival
- Pita Kitchen
- Saffy's restaurant
- Sham el Nessim springtime celebrations
- Sumac Mediterranean
- The Falafel Factory Food Truck
- The Halal Guys
- The Original Hawowshi
- Tut's Grill & Catering
- West LA International Market

Organizations And Institutions

- Consulate General of the Arab Republic of Egypt
- Egyptian American Organization
- Egyptians in Los Angeles Facebook Group
- Ernie Wolfe Gallery
- Fowler Museum at UCLA Mellon African Art Initiative
- Getty Villa Museum
- King Fahad Mosque
- Los Angeles County Museum of Art Egyptian Art Collection
- Museum of Jurassic Technology Hagop Sandaldjian exhibit
- Rele Art Gallery
- St. Mark Coptic Orthodox Church
- Yalla Egyptian American Collective

Egyptian

California has the largest representation of Arab Americans in the country and—you guessed it—Los Angeles has the largest share of that population. There is a strong Egyptian presence in the Orange County area, which is also where you will find Little Arabia, but Los Angeles has some uniquely Egyptian experiences, too. Probably the most well-known presence in Los Angeles are The Halal Guys—Egyptian fast food joints that have been popping up all over the country. Meanwhile, the most famous venue in Hollywood would be the Egyptian Theatre, which features an Egyptian Revival style of architecture, the result of a popular fascination with Egyptian archaeology in the 1920s unrelated to the Egyptian culture as such.

The Original Hawowshi is an Egyptian street food pop-up offering hawowshi and feteer. *Credit: Amir Edward*

Also along Hollywood Boulevard are the historic El Capitan Theatre, Grauman's Chinese Theatre, Ovation Hollywood Mall, and Hollywood Roosevelt Hotel. A little farther away from the sights and sounds is the Magic Castle—one of those venues where only members and invited guests can visit.

For halal and vegan Egyptian cuisine, Amir Edward's The Original Hawowshi is the spot. *Credit: Amir Edward*

Ethiopian

You know you are in Little Ethiopia when these banners pop up everywhere.
Credit: Ruksana Hussain

Little Ethiopia is your destination to satisfy any tibs (stir fry) and injera (fermented pancake) cravings. It isn't the only place you can find the Ethiopian community and food in Los Angeles, but it is your best bet. The area on Fairfax Avenue, officially designated in 2002, can be easily identified by the Little Ethiopia banners on the lampposts. There are enough restaurants that if one is too busy, another will welcome you. After restaurant-hopping, you can also go shopping—there are vintage and thrift stores here as well as markets that showcase Ethiopian products. If you continue along from Fairfax Avenue toward La Brea then you will hit the Miracle Mile, which is also called Museum Row. The La Brea Tar Pits and Page Museum, Los Angeles County Museum of Art (locally known as LACMA), and the Craft Contemporary are all here.

If museums aren't your thing, then historic Beverly Cinema on Beverly Boulevard isn't too far either—it is THE place to watch a movie from filmmaker Quentin Tarantino's personal collection. End back in Little Ethiopia for some tej (honey wine), araki (flavored liqueur), or flavorful Ethiopian coffee.

Food And Celebrations

African Restaurant Week

Aunt Yvette's Kitchen

Awash

Berbere by T&T Lifestyle

Betty Market

Buna Market

Cantaloop

Easter and Christmas celebrations

Eid and Ramadan celebrations

Emma Habesha

Flavors from Afar

Industry Café & Jazz

Lalibela

Little Ethiopia New Year Festival

Lucy

Meals by Genet

Melkam

Merkato

Messob

Omar's

Pan African Film and Arts Festival

Paradocs Coffee

Queen of Sheba

Rahel Vegan

Rosalind's

Yordanos

Organizations And Institutions

African American Cultural Center

Amanuel Ethiopian Church

Ernie Wolfe Gallery

Ethiopian Christian Fellowship Church

Ethiopian Community Los Angeles

Fowler Museum at UCLA Mellon African Art Initiative

Islamic Center of Los Angeles

Islamic Center of Southern California

Jewish Federation Los Angeles

Little Ethiopia Business Association

Little Ethiopia Cultural and Resource Center

Los Angeles County Museum of Art African Art Collection

Rele Art Gallery

Virgin Mary Ethiopian Orthodox Tewahedo Church

Zawadi Cultural Collective

Food And Celebrations

Aquarium of the Pacific Southeast Asia Day festival

Asian American and Pacific Islander Heritage Month in May

Bone Kettle Restaurant

Dollar Hits Filipino Streetfood

Ensaymada Project

Festival of Philippine Arts and Culture

Fiesta Barbecue and Bibingka

HiFi Kitchen

Historic Filipinotown Parol Parade

Independence Day celebrations in June

K&R Grill

Kuya Lord

Lasita

Manila Inasal

Mano Po

Simbang Gabi Christmas celebration

Spoon and Pork

The Park's Finest

Organizations And Institutions

FilAm Arts

Filipino American Community of Los Angeles Facebook group

Filipino American Service Group Bayanihan Center

Historic Filipinotown

Kayamanan Ng Lahi Philippine Folk Arts

Los Angeles County Library Asian Pacific Resource Center

Los Angeles County Museum of Art South and Southeast Asian Art Collection

Malaya Filipino American Dance Arts

UCLA Center for Southeast Asian Studies

Westside Christian Church Tagalog Ministries

Filipino

Historic Filipinotown or HiFi is another ethnic enclave in Los Angeles. The name is more reflective of the fact that this is where many Filipinos first settled when migrating than because of a majority presence in the area. Located here is Echo Park Lake, a major neighborhood attraction where evenings and weekends can get busy.

Filipino dishes like chicken inasal are easily available at LA restaurants. *Credit: Ruksana Hussain*

Away from the park, you can walk along the streets where HiFi has many shopping and dining options. Look for the Gintong Kasaysayan, a huge mural tribute to Filipinos everywhere. It is the largest Filipino American mural in the United States and consists of two parts—one that is historical and another that's contemporary. Also located here are the historic Filipino arch/sign and the World War II Veterans Monument. The city's Department of Cultural Affairs has a downloadable map for a self-guided tour of all the historic points of interest. When finished, head back to the lake for a picnic—street vendors are always around and it's open seating on the grass—or rent a swan boat to pedal out on the lake and take in views from the other side. Sunset is the perfect time to be here.

French

Escargot platter at Shirley Brasserie at Hollywood Roosevelt Hotel. *Credit: Shirley Brasserie*

Given how easy it is to find a French café or bistro to dine in, you'd assume there's a Little Paris or some other specifically designated French Quarter in Los Angeles. No such luck. Though the French community was once an integral part of the city, the population has dispersed across several neighborhoods now and the only signs of French history per se are the names on some of the street signs and the Art Deco buildings of downtown. The LA Conservancy has an Art Deco Walking Tour that takes you to historic spots in the downtown area, including those with French connections. Some of the well-known Art Deco structures include the Central Library, Pantages Theatre, Griffith Observatory, Jewelry Center, and the Wiltern Theatre. Other landmarks with French architecture include Chateau Elysee located in Hollywood, a replica of a French chateau now owned by the Church of Scientology. Chateau Marmont, a hotel and restaurant in the Hollywood area, is also designed after a French chateau, and The French Chateau apartment building is also listed as a Historic Cultural Monument. You could spend a whole day looking at all these French influences, then go indulge in French cuisine afterward. Bon appetit!

The Arts District's Le Champ is a Parisian-inspired neighborhood wine bar. *Credit: Le Champ*

Food And Celebrations

A Food Affair

Amandine Patisserie Café

American French Film Festival

Bar Chelou

Café Stella

Camphor

Compagnon Wine Bistro

Kiff Kafe

Kendall's Brasserie

L'appart

La Provence Patisserie and Café LAX

Le Champ

Le Petit Jardin

Le Petit Paris

Le Sanglier

Loupiotte Kitchen

Lumiere

Mignon Wine Bar

Mistral

Monsieur Marcel Gourmet Market & Bistro

Mr. T

Oriel Chinatown

Perch

Petit Trois

Pitchoun!

Republique

Shirley Brasserie

Taix

Organizations And Institutions

Alliance Française French Language and Cultural Center

Armand Hammer Daumier and Contemporaries Collection

Art Deco Society of Los Angeles

Consulate General of France in Los Angeles

Franco American Cultural Fund

French Heart Jazz Band

French Heritage Society Southern California

Los Angeles County Museum of Art European Painting and Sculpture Collection

Los Angeles Walking Tours

Praz-Delavallade Gallery

St. Sebastian's Catholic Church

The French Apartment Gallery

The Huntington Library European Art Collection

Wally's Wines

Food And Celebrations

- Aldi Grocery Store
- Ashland Hill
- Austrian American Day
- Berlin Currywurst
- Berlins Doner Kebab
- Biergarten LA
- Black Forest Bakery
- Dog Haus Biergarten
- German American Heritage Month
- German Currents Film Festival
- Idle Hour Bar
- Krampus Nights
- Lustig
- Oktoberfest
- Red Lion Tavern
- Rockenwagner Bakery + Market
- Schreiner's Fine Sausages
- The Berlin Truck
- The Museum of Jurassic Technology Athanasius Kircher exhibit
- Two Coast Brewing
- Vienna Pastry
- Wirtshaus Biergarten
- World Market
- Wurstkuche

Organizations And Institutions

- Bayern Club
- California Germans
- Da Stube Buben Folk Music
- Deutscher Stammtisch Los Angeles
- Donauschwäbische Tanzgruppe
- First German UMC/ Christuskirche
- G.T.E.V. D'Oberlandler
- German American Club of Santa Monica
- German American League
- German Consulate General
- Goethe Institut
- Hammerstein Band Musik Bavaria
- Hazelnuss Band
- LACMA Rifkind Center for German Expressionist Studies
- Los Angeles Soccer Club
- Los Angeles Turners
- Schindler House
- The Bluebirds Showband
- UCLA Department of European Languages and Transcultural Studies
- Villa Aurora

German/Austrian

The Villa Aurora is the former home of German-Jewish author Lion Feuchtwanger and his wife Marta.
Credit: Joshua White

Austrian-born American architect Rudolph Michael Schindler left his mark on LA with the list of Historic Cultural Monuments built from his designs. They include Laurelwood Apartments in Studio City and the Tischler Residence in Westwood. The only church he designed was the Bethlehem Baptist Church in the Central Alameda district. His Schindler House now serves as the headquarters for the MAK Center for Art and Architecture which presents tours and is listed on the US National Register of Historic Places.

Another Austrian American who left his mark on LA is Richard Joseph Neutra, known for his modernist style. His Neutra Office Building in Silver Lake is also a Historic Cultural Monument and on the National Register of Historic Places. In addition, his Neutra VDL Studio and Residences where he lived was eventually donated to Cal Poly for its College of Environmental Design. The Silver Lake area houses several Neutra designs, and you can find architecture tours that take you through these sites. Also found in Silver Lake are the Silver Lake Reservoir (great walking loop trail, wth a dog park nearby) and Elysian Park (known for its hiking trails), located close to Dodger Stadium.

The Schindler House was designed over a two-month period in 1921.
Credit: Tag Christof

Ghanaian

African Chop Food Truck's fare includes Cameroonian flavors.
Credit: African Chop Food Truck

Ghanaian art and food are easily accessible in Los Angeles. The Ernie Wolfe Gallery in Sawtelle and The Museum of African American Art in Baldwin Hills Crenshaw Plaza have often spotlighted work from Ghana, and Ghanaian artists have shown at galleries and museums in LA. In early 2024, the Fowler Museum at UCLA permanently repatriated to the Asante Kingdom seven objects forcibly taken by the British in 1874, and the museum plans to create replicas for display instead so public education and awareness of the history of the continent continues. Meanwhile, Ghanaian festivals provide avenues for experiencing the culture, food, and community in the city. And though Cameroonian, the folks behind African Chop Food Truck are introducing West African cuisine to events and venues where Angelenos and visitors can savor creations such as wild-caught mackerel, suya (meat skewers), spinach, puff puffs (fried dough), and more. There are plenty of other spots where you can enjoy Ghanaian cuisine, or you can learn to make the dishes at home with private Chef Afia Anabasua who also hosts community suppers and cooking demos at several locations in the city.

African Chop Food Truck serves West African cuisine in Los Angeles.
Credit: African Chop Food Truck

Food And Celebrations

- Aduke Cuisine and Lounge
- African Chop Food Truck
- African Obichi Food Store
- African Restaurant Week
- Black History Month Festival celebrations
- Dat Moi Market
- Ghanaian Independence Day celebrations
- Gloria's Shito
- Homowo festival
- Minaco Ventures African Food Market
- Nkechi African Cafe
- Pan African Film and Arts Festival
- Sumptuous African Restaurant
- Sweet Jollof
- The Peppered Goat
- Two Hommes
- Ubuntu Vegan
- Veronica's Kitchen
- Weaf restaurant

Organizations And Institutions

- African American Cultural Center
- Art + Practice
- California African American Museum
- Dembrebrah West African Drum & Dance Ensemble
- Ernie Wolfe Gallery
- Fowler Museum at UCLA Mellon African Art Initiative
- Ghana Association of Southern California
- Inner City Cultural Center
- Los Angeles County Museum of Art African Art Collection
- Lula Washington Dance Theater
- Malik Books
- Presbyterian Church of Ghana Southern California
- Rele Art Gallery
- The Broad
- The William Grant Still Arts Center
- Zawadi Cultural Collective

Food And Celebrations

- Aliki's Taverna
- Café Santorini
- Elena's Estiatorio
- Great Greek
- Kalamaki Fine Greek Street Food
- Long Beach Greek Food and Music Festival
- Los Angeles Greek Fest
- Los Angeles Greek Film Festival
- Meat the Greek
- Mykonos Greek Grill
- Nick the Greek
- South Bay Greek Festival
- South East European Film Festival
- St. George Greek Festival
- Taverna at the Mar Vista
- Taverna Tony Greek Eats and Sweets
- The Great Greek Restaurant Taverna
- Valley Greek Festival

Organizations And Institutions

- California Greeks
- Getty Villa Museum
- Greek Consulate General
- Los Angeles County Museum of Art Greek, Roman and Etruscan Art Collection
- Saint George Greek Orthodox Church
- Saint Nicholas Greek Orthodox Church
- Southern California Cretans' Association
- UCLA Stavros Niarchos Foundation Center for the Study of Hellenic Culture

Greek

The community that was Greek Town in the downtown area has moved out over time and dispersed across the city and county. The Byzantine-Latino Quarter on Pico Boulevard has since become a much more diverse space. Despite this mini-diaspora, LA still has one of the larger Greek populations outside of Greece and you will find myriad ways to experience the culture, including restaurants and festivals for enjoying the food, music, and arts. The Greek Theatre is an LA must-see for its Greek Revival architectural design. It is considered a more intimate venue for performance viewing than the Hollywood Bowl. Other attractions nearby include Griffith Observatory (look for the Berendo stairs for a memorable hike), the American Film Institute, Ennis-Brown House by Frank Lloyd Wright, Silverlake Conservatory of Music, and the Vermonica artwork installation—where LA vintage streetlamps have found an afterlife. The LA Greek Fest is a three-day affair celebrating all things Greek food, culture, and entertainment, as is the Long Beach Greek Food and Music Festival. Note those fall dates in your plans if you'd like a one-stop destination to enjoy all things Greek in LA.

The Great Greek was the celebration location of the movie *My Big Fat Greek Wedding 3.*
Credit: The Great Greek

Kalamaki Greek LA's Greek Frozen Yogurt comes topped with baklava.
Credit: Kalamaki Greek LA

Guatemalan

Baked goods and sweet treats are plenty at any Guatemalan bakery.
Credit: Ruksana Hussain

Angelenos in the know will tell you that the Guatemalan night markets in the Westlake area are the spot to visit for the variety of street food and vendors. If you watched Anthony Bourdain's Little Guatemala episode on the CNN show *Explore Parts Unknown*, you get the picture. However, if you can't get to the markets, there are several Guatemalan bakeries and restaurants tucked away in strip malls across the city. Although some are more modest than others, the food is just as good and service equally friendly in each one. Aside from food, the arts are a big part of Guatemalan Angeleno culture so look for works by artists such as Andrea Sofia Santizo and the artist Cache, who also goes by Chicken Man (you'll understand the name when you see his artwork around the city). While there isn't an official murals tour, a well-researched, self-guided one is feasible. Finally, the Guatemala County Fair in Grand Park, a two-day event held in the summer, is one big all-are-welcome party where food, arts, music, and dance come together. Other festive occasions to mark your calendars for are Afro-Latinx Festival, Central American Festival and Parade, and Festival Chapin.

Food And Celebrations

Afro-Latinx Festival

Antigua Coffee House

Aquarium of the Pacific Noche de Estrellas

Café Chapin Guatemalteco

Casa Chapina Restaurant

Central American Festival and Parade

El Carrusel Bakery

Festival Chapin

Garifuna International Indigenous Film Festival

Garifuna Settlement Day Mass

Garnachas and Beer Restaurant

Guatemalteca Bakery

Guatetoto Restaurant

Mi Cocinita Chapina

National Hispanic Heritage Month

Pan y Comida Guatemalteca Channys

Panaderia Guatepan

Puchica Guatemalan Bar & Grill

Rositas Guate-Mex Restaurant

Shucos L.A Sabor Chapin

Organizations And Institutions

Avenue 50 Studio

Bilingual Foundation of the Arts

Casa de la Cultura de Guatemala Los Angeles

Central American Confederation

Consulate General of Guatemala

Garifuna American Heritage Foundation United

Garifuna Museum of Los Angeles

Ix'iq Designs

LaPau Gallery

Latino Outdoors

Latino Theater Company

Los Angeles County Museum of Art's Art of the Ancient Americas and Latin America

Museum of Latin American Art

The Broad

The Floricanto Center for the Performing Arts

Translatina Coalition

Food And Celebrations

Annual Kahanamoku Klassic Outrigger Canoe Race

Aquarium of the Pacific's Pacific Islander Festival

Asian American and Pacific Islander Heritage Month in May

Asian Pacific Film Festival

Belles Beach House

Canoe House

Fiyahnesian Pacific Island Fusion Street Cuisine

Hapa Day celebrations

Heritage of Aloha Festival

Kahuna Tiki Restaurant & Tiki Lounge

Manini Kine Grindz

Poasa Imports Samoan Market

Poly Grill and Bakery

Shrimp Daddy at Topanga Social

The Los Angeles Pasifika Film Festival

Tiki No Bar

Tiki-Ti Bar

Tonga Hut

Organizations And Institutions

Blue13 Dance Company

Coalition of Asian Pacifics in Entertainment

Coco Tiki Entertainment

Craft Contemporary

Fiji Indians Los Angeles

Guava Groove Ukulele Classes

Heart of Samba Entertainment

Los Angeles County Library Asian Pacific Resource Center

OCI Polynesian Store

Ohana Ukuleles

Pacific Island Ethnic Art Museum

Polynesian Paradise Dancers

South Bay Strummers

The Ho'Oilina Foundation

Hawaiian/ Pacific Islander

There is a large Pacific Islander community in Los Angeles. Several festivals are hosted across the county—like the Heritage of Aloha and Outrigger Canoe Race—and bring the community together. Other events include the Alondra Park Ho'olaule'a, the Aloha Beach Festival in Ventura, the Ukulele Festival in Los Angeles, and the Southern California Slack Key Festival in Redondo Beach. And that's just to get started. The Pacific Island Ethnic Art Museum provides an opportunity to view the arts and learn the stories of many islands in one venue. The University of Southern California's Pacific Asia Museum features decorative and folk arts. Other museums in the county have limited-engagement exhibits that are regularly made available to the public and are well-attended. The options for dining at Hawaiian BBQ spots, poke cafes, and tiki bars in LA are too many to list here but hope you enjoy some of the recommendations on the opposite page for rounding out your festival experience.

Experience the aloha spirit and island culture of Hawaii at Kahuna Tiki Restaurant & Tiki Lounge. *Credit: Jack Rabbit Flash*

Visit Kahuna Tiki Restaurant & Tiki Lounge for its South Pacific island-style atmosphere. *Credit: Jack Rabbit Flash*

Honduran

Tour guide Cynthia Lewis with traditional drums at Garifuna Museum of Los Angeles. *Credit: Media Marathon*

When *Ugly Betty* made its debut starring actress America Ferrera, the show turned a spotlight on the Los Angeles Honduran community. As more viewers followed Betty's journey, they were also drawn to Ferrera's breakthrough moment in her acting career. Over the years, the Honduran presence in the city has grown, making it one of the larger Central American populations in LA. With that came more restaurants, festivals, and other cultural events, including the Central American Festival and Parade and the Afro-Latinx Festival in Long Beach. The latest addition is the Garifuna Museum of Los Angeles, which is doing its part to showcase the Garifuna people and their culture, preserve their community, and share their history. A guided tour (by appointment only) takes visitors through three galleries of arts and artifacts of importance to the Garifuna people.

Alfonso Cayetano at Garifuna Museum of Los Angeles, which showcases Garifuna life. *Credit: Media Marathon*

Food And Celebrations

- Aquarium of the Pacific Noche de Estrellas
- Casa Honduras Los Ángeles restaurant
- Central American Festival and Parade
- Copan Sula Restaurant
- Dat Moi Market
- Doña Bibi's Restaurant
- El Katracho Honduran Restaurant
- El Sazón K-tracho #3
- Expo Hondureña USA
- Garifuna International Indigenous Film Festival
- Garifuna Settlement Day Mass
- Honduras Kitchen – La Casa de la Sopa de Caracol
- La Troca Catracha
- Museum of Latin American Art Afro-Latinx Festival
- National Hispanic Heritage Month
- Rincón Hondureño

Organizations And Institutions

- Bilingual Foundation of the Arts
- Broad American Art Museum Latin American Art Collection
- Central American Confederation
- Consulate General of Honduras
- Garifuna American Heritage Foundation United
- Garifuna Museum of Los Angeles
- Heart of Samba Entertainment
- Museum of Latin American Art
- The Broad

Food And Celebrations

Babushka Deli

Celebration of Hanukkah: Festival of Lights in December

Christmas celebrations

EuroAsia Restaurant

European Deli Market

Hungarian Film Festival of Los Angeles

Kiff Kafe

Mechta International Deli

Mom, Please Ukrainian Food

Monta Factory

Oliv'e Food Market

Otto's European and Hungarian Import Store & Deli

Pacific Coast Food

Pirozzi's Italian Deli

Posto896

Sebastian's Mediterranean

South East European Film Festival

Strada Eateria and Bar

Sunset Grill Hollywood

West LA International Market

Organizations And Institutions

Consulate General of Hungary

Grace Hungarian Reformed Church

Hungarian Cultural Alliance

Hungarians on the West Coast

Karpatok Hungarian Dance Ensemble

Los Angeles County Museum of Art European Painting and Sculpture Collection

Los Angeles Public Library International Languages Department

Saint Stephen's Catholic Church

Skirball Cultural Center

Wende Museum

Hungarian

One of the earliest Hungarians to achieve fame in Hollywood was actress Zsa Zsa Gabor, who took the industry by storm. She was one of the first international stars whose name appeared on the Hollywood Walk of Fame and tourists are still spotted taking pictures of her star. Gabor lived to be almost 100 and her passing was mourned in LA.

Nokedli (dumpling) with beef stew or chicken paprikash is a Hungarian staple.
Credit: Ruksana Hussain

Today, most Hungarians live in the Westside and in the San Fernando Valley. Culturally, however, the community is very active, getting together to celebrate with film festivals and holidays. The Hungarian Cultural Alliance hosts performances and other events for the community. There aren't many Hungarian restaurants or community clubs (the usual venues where most people can find out about a new-to-you culture), but one can find an array of Hungarian and Italian dishes lovingly prepared at Posto896. Any other venues with Hungarian fare provide more of a mélange of cuisines rather than specific Hungarian dishes.

Indian

Munna Bhai MBBS cocktail at Baar Baar LA where the cocktails are named after Bollywood movies. *Credit: Neil John Burger*

The Indian community is represented in the Orange County area but also in cities such as Artesia where Little India comprises several Indian groceries, department stores, and restaurants offering a myriad of regional Indian cuisines. Indian festivals and celebrations occur across the larger Los Angeles metro area and visiting during festival seasons ensures culinary delicacies at almost every Indian eatery there is. The Malibu Hindu Temple is a well-known landmark and one structure that's hard to miss given its unique architectural style. Another venue to visit is the Mahatma Gandhi World Peace Memorial in the beautiful meditation gardens of the Lake Shrine Self-Realization Fellowship Temple. The Southern California Cricket Club and Los Angeles Cricket groups foster love for India's favorite sport in the City of Angels. Several celebrities with Indian origins live in Los Angeles; in fact, the first South Asian immigrant ever to become a US citizen was an Angeleno—Indian-born Eduljee Sorabjee, a Parsi from Mumbai, in 1890. Coincidentally, Mumbai is a sister city to Los Angeles.

Kapoor's Akbar Indian Food has been serving greater LA for over three decades. *Credit: Avinash Kapoor*

Food And Celebrations

- 23rd Street Café
- Abhiruchi Grill
- Agra Café
- Anar
- Arth Culver City
- Baar Baar LA
- Badmaash
- Biriyani Kabob House
- Delhi Belly
- Diwali and Holi celebrations
- Eid and Ramadan celebrations
- Electric Karma
- Flavor of India
- India Sweets and Spices
- India's Grill
- Indian Film Festival
- Jaipur Cuisine of India
- Kapoor's Akbar
- Mayura
- Mr. Masala
- Nizam of India
- Roots Bistro
- Samosa House
- Shor
- Star of India Tandoori
- Tulsi Eatery

Organizations And Institutions

- Artesia City Church
- Bhagavad-Gita Museum
- Blue13 Dance Company
- Guru Ram Das Ashram
- Hollywood Sikh Temple
- Hosanna International Church
- India Association of Los Angeles
- International Society for Krishna Consciousness
- Islamic Center of Southern California
- ISSO Shree Swaminarayan Temple
- Khalsa Care Foundation
- King Fahad Mosque
- Soorya Foundation for Performing Arts
- Southern California Cricket Association
- The Norton Simon Museum South and Southeast Asian Painting and Sculpture Collection

Food And Celebrations

- Asia Supermarket
- Asian American and Pacific Islander Heritage Month in May
- Awan Dessert Shop
- Blasteran Beverly Hills
- Bone Kettle Restaurant
- Borneo Kalimantan Cuisine
- Bungkus Bagus
- Cobi's
- Indo Bistro
- LaaLaaPan
- Los Angeles Indonesian Film Festival
- Medan Kitchen
- Mee and Greet
- Merry's House of Chicken
- Mr. Sate restaurant
- Mutiara Halal Food and Market
- Noodle Stars
- Plus62 Street Food
- Satay Indonesian Delights
- Simpang Asia Restaurant
- Stop Bye Café Indonesian Fusion Food Truck
- Toko Rame
- Uncle Fung Borneo Eatery
- Wallflower
- Wayang Restaurant

Organizations And Institutions

- CalArts Balinese and Javanese Music and Dance
- Consulate General of the Republic of Indonesia
- Indonesia Muslim Foundation At-Thohir Center
- Indonesian American SDA Church Azusa
- Los Angeles County Library Asian Pacific Resource Center
- Los Angeles County Museum of Art South and Southeast Asian Art Collection
- SoCal Indo Facebook group
- The Norton Simon Museum South and Southeast Asian Painting and Sculpture Collection
- USC Fisher Museum of Art
- USC Pacific Asia Museum

Indonesian

Mee and Greet's Laksa Chicken Noodle served with housemade spicy coconut noodle broth.
Credit: Mee and Greet

Indonesians, despite being a large population in Los Angeles, do not have an ethnic enclave like Thai Town or Koreatown. But don't let that hold you back from pursuing a hot plate of nasi goreng (fried rice with meat and vegetables) or beef rendang (dark stew made with slow-cooked beef). The community might be dispersed but the food is very much available in the city. Just look at the number of options listed here and know that this isn't even scratching the surface. Indonesian fusion fare is widely available as well—keep an eye out for venues that advertise that option. From food trucks to dessert shops, every neighborhood has several spots to explore. Given the city's fair weather, it is easy to find a spot on a patio or rooftop because Los Angeles takes its outdoor dining seriously. There are entire lists dedicated to finding the best spots with gorgeous city views, but a good bet is to ask some locals familiar with the area and you might just find a hidden gem.

Find sambal tuna and mee goreng at Chef Justin's StopBye Food Truck – The Original Indonesian Fusion
Credit: StopBye Food Truck.

Iranian

Persian Gulf in Westwood is a museum/ restaurant serving history and food.
Credit: Persian Gulf

Westwood, on the Westside, is locally known as Little Persia for its large Iranian presence, although there is no official designation. However, there is official signage for Persian Square. Los Angeles has the largest Iranian population outside of Iran, earning LA the monikers Tehrangeles or Irangeles.

LA Conservancy offers visitors a guide for neighborhoods where the Iranian community lives called "Irangeles: A Driving Tour," which includes Reseda, Woodland Hills, Encino, and the Pico-Robertson area. During Nowruz, the annual new year celebration, you'll see festivities galore, and the Farhang Foundation hosts a charming annual Nowruz celebration that is open to the public. Programming usually includes a concert that is also well-attended. Los Angeles also boasts several Iranian American artists among its residents, including tar/sitar player and composer Fariborz Azizi. Several LA-area museums regularly include Iranian arts and exhibits but a trip to West Hollywood's Iranian-owned Advocartsy gallery promoting Iranian artists is highly recommended. Aside from a plethora of Iranian and Persian eateries, expect to see many kosher Iranian spots as well since Los Angeles is home to a sizable Jewish Iranian population.

At Toranj, traditional Iranian dishes served include loubia polo and fesenjoon.
Credit: Toranj

Food And Celebrations

Asal Bakery
Cabaret Tehran
Café Glace
Chelo Taste of Persia
Darya
Elat Market
Farhang Foundation Nowruz celebrations
Jino's Pars
Kabob by Faraj
Kinrose Creamery
Kourosh
Kouzeh Bakery
Mashti Malone's Ice Cream
Massis Kabob
Persian Gulf
Pink Orchid Bakery & Café
Raffi's Place
Sadaf
Saffron & Rose Ice Cream
Sasoun Bakery
Sasoun Produce
Shamshiri Grill
Shekarchi Mediterranean
Shirin
Sofreh
Tajrish Persian
Taste of Tehran
Tehran Market grocery store
Toranj Restaurant
Urth Caffé
West LA International Market

Organizations And Institutions

Century City Freedom Sculpture
Farhang Foundation
Iranian American Jewish Federation
Iranian American Muslim Association of North America
Iranian American Womens Foundation LA Chapter
Ketab Bookstore
Los Angeles County Museum Art of the Middle East Collection
Mansour Tapestries
Mediterranean Market at Farmers Market
Pourdavoud Institute
UCLA Center for Near Eastern Studies
UCLA Sephardic Archive Initiative
West LA International Market
Younes and Soraya Nazarian Center for the Performing Arts

Iranian: The annual Nowruz celebration at UCLA is a gathering for the Iranian community but also all of Los Angeles. *Credit: Farhang Foundation and Vafa Khatami*

Food And Celebrations

- Akkad Mediterranean and Iraqi Grill
- Al Basch Chicken
- Ammatoli
- Arab American Heritage Month celebrations in April
- Borjstar Shawarma Shop
- Bowery Bungalow
- Easter and Christmas celebrations
- Eid and Ramadan celebrations
- Galata Halal Eatery
- Glendale Shawarma
- Kebab Halebi
- Koko's
- Mush Bakery Nawal
- New Arrival Supper Club
- NewFilmmakers Los Angeles Film Festival InFocus: Middle Eastern & Arab Cinema
- The Chee Legacy
- West LA International Market
- World Refugee Day

Organizations And Institutions

- Famous Stage Productions
- Iraqi Consulate General in Los Angeles
- Jewish Federation Los Angeles
- Kahal Joseph Congregation
- Los Angeles County Museum Art of the Middle East Collection
- Los Angeles Public Library International Languages Department
- Masjid Al-Zahra
- Middle Eastern Events Los Angeles
- NewFilmmakers Los Angeles NFMLA Monthly Film Festival InFocus: Middle Eastern & Arab Cinema
- Qabila Foundation
- UCLA Sephardic Archive Initiative

Iraqi

In Glendale, Akkad offers a delicious Iraqi lamb shish teka. *Credit: Ruksana Hussain*

There is a large representation of Arab Americans in Los Angeles and California, including immigrants from Lebanon, Egypt, and Iraq, which only means more cultural experiences of and exposure to new music, art, and cuisine. For a taste of Iraqi food, Akkad Mediterranean and Iraqi Grill has delicacies such as soujouk (sausage), kahi (puff pastry with syrup), and a variety of kebabs and stews. When it comes to the performing arts, local companies and visiting acts provide a few options. Famous Stage Productions hosts performances in both Los Angeles and Orange counties, and comics such as Paul Elia and Yaseen Mazin provide entertaining insights into their Iraqi backgrounds and upbringing. The Middle Eastern Events Los Angeles group on Facebook shares details on upcoming concerts and other community events.

There is also a large Iraqi Jewish presence in LA and the Jewish Federation organizes events to bring the community together. The Iraqi community brings with it another chance for Angelenos and visitors to tune in and absorb a whole new experience of living in this city. So here's to learning more about traditional music genres and dance styles like maqam and kawleeya, calligraphy, and other art forms from the Iraqi culture.

Irish

The Cat and Fiddle hosts fun St. Patrick's Day events every year. *Credit: Oscar Jimenez*

St. Patrick's Day provides many opportunities to discover the Irish influences in Los Angeles. A quick search online yields St. Patrick's Day pub crawls, parades, and other special events but there is also a Lucky Run to earn your whiskey and stew. The Original Farmers Market also celebrates the day with music and food as do many other venues. While you won't see an officially designated Irish stronghold in any part of the city, you will probably find several Irish pubs—sometimes just minutes from each other. If an Irish coffee is on the agenda, there are many options available. Los Angeles also has whiskey and beer festivals during the year, so you are sure to find one with an Irish theme. In fact, food festivals can be found around LA almost every month, even if they do not pertain to a particular culture or community. There's the Vegan Street Fair, Valley Food Truck Fest, Masters of Taste, and many more food festivals. Weekly events include "Smorgasburg" (every Sunday) and neighborhood farmers' markets, too. And if you'd like a few Irish products to take home then Kitty O'Shea's Irish and UK Market presents a wide variety.

Not Irish, but Tam O'Shanter Scottish pub is a must-visit steakhouse. *Credit: Jakob Layman*

Food And Celebrations

Dublin's Whiskey Pub

Forman's Whiskey Tavern

Griffins of Kinsale

Ireland Week

Irish American Heritage Month celebrations in March

Jameson's Sports Grill

Kitty O'Shea's Irish and UK Market

Molly Malone's

Reilly's Irish Pub

Seven Grand Whiskey Society

St. Paddy's Day Lucky Run

St. Patrick's Day Parade

St. Patrick's Day Pub Crawl

The Big Irish Fair and Music Festival

The Cat and Fiddle

The Irish Film Festival LA

The Irish Times

The Liberties of Dublin

The Tam O'Shanter

Tom Bergin's

Organizations And Institutions

Celtic Irish Dance Academy

City of Angels Pipe Band

Clearly Irish Dance Pasadena

Consulate General of Ireland

Contemporary Irish Arts Center

Kerry Irish Productions

Los Angeles County Museum of Art European Painting and Sculpture Collection

Los Angeles Hurling Club

Los Angeles Police Emerald Society Pipes and Drums

McNulty School of Irish Dance

The Celtic Arts Center of Southern California

The Irish Center of Southern California

Food And Celebrations

Amiga Amore

Angelini Osteria

Barrique

Bestia

Ca'Del Sole

Cento

Day of the Drum Festival

DeSano Pizza Bakery

Felix Trattoria

Forma

Italia Film, Fashion and Art Fest

Italian American Heritage Month in October

Jemma di Mare

La Pergoletta Deli

Maggiano's Little Italy

Mother Wolf

Osteria La Buca

Osteria Mamma

Pasta e Pasta by Allegro

Pasta Sisters

Rafaello Ristorante

Scopa Italian Roots

Taste of Italy

The Factory Kitchen

The Los Angeles Italian Festival

Watts Tower Jazz Festival

Organizations And Institutions

Annual Grand Gala Carnevale Masquerade Ball

Consulate General of Italy

Getty Villa Museum

Guidi Marcello

Italian American Club of San Pedro

Italian American Museum

Italian Cultural Institute of Los Angeles

Italy Run

Little Italy District

Little Italy of Los Angeles Association

Los Angeles County Museum of Art Greek, Roman and Etruscan Art Collection

Maestro Sausage Company

Opera Italia

San Antonio Winery

St. Peter's Italian Church

Watts Tower Arts Center

Italian

Although most of the Italian population in Los Angeles lives in coastal San Pedro, several areas retain an Italian/European flavor in downtown LA. St. Vincent Court, downtown off 7th Street in the Jewelry District, showcases European-style shops lining the street for a distinctly Italian feel. The Getty Villa Museum in Pacific Palisades is modeled after an ancient Roman villa and has gorgeous Italian antiquities collections on display. The Venice Canal Historic District in the LA suburbs was modeled on those romantic waterways of Venice, Italy. The Italian Hall downtown in the former unofficial Little Italy is now the premises for the Italian American Museum. Italian American-owned San Antonio Winery is the only one out of more than 90 wineries that survived Prohibition and is now a thriving venue with tastings and tours available.

Forma in Venice is named after formaggio, the star ingredient at this venue. *Credit: Forma*

For those who prefer beer, the Brewery Art Walk is only a short stroll away. Stop by Watts Tower, built by Italian immigrant and construction worker Sabato Rodia over a leisurely 30-odd years. The tower is a National Historic Landmark and visitors can experience a guided tour here or attend any of the cultural events at the Watts Tower Arts Campus.

Italian : Try the scallop aguachile at Mexican Italian spot Amiga Amore.
Credit: Amiga Amore

Food And Celebrations

- Ackee Bamboo
- Bridgetown Roti
- Caribbean American Heritage Month celebrations in June
- Caribbean Heritage Festival
- Cha Cha Chicken
- Da Jerk Yard
- Dulan's on Crenshaw
- Fayah Sundays
- Hungry Joe's
- Island Boy Café
- Jamaican Gold
- Los Angeles Carnival
- Los Angeles Culture Festival Hollywood Carnival
- Natraliart
- Now Serving
- Ozi's Kitchen
- Reggae Fest
- Rubie
- Sattdown Grill
- The Original Coleys
- Wah Gwaan Kitchen and Bar
- Wi Jammin
- Yaad Vibes Island Cuisine

Organizations And Institutions

- Afro-Latin & Afro-Caribbean Community of California Facebook group
- Arise Roots
- Caribbean Heritage Organization
- Dread Daze
- Jahmark & the Soulshakers
- Jamaica Cultural Alliance
- Jamaican Awareness Association
- Reggae Love LA
- Right Choice Caribbean Market
- Rivera Produce Corporation
- The Room Hollywood
- Upstream Music

Jamaican

Jamaica often invokes thoughts of reggae and rum, and the city of Los Angeles celebrates those Caribbean contributions with a rum festival every year while reggae is celebrated in Long Beach—both areas with vibrant Caribbean, including Jamaican, populations. Both festivals deliver lots of good food, fun celebrations, and multiple ways to experience the culture. The Caribbean American Heritage Foundation has been instrumental in hosting such events in the city including the annual music and arts fest and the Carnaval Parade.

Bridgetown Roti by Chef Rashida Holmes offers Caribbean American food.
Credit: Kennedy Clark

Craving Jamaican comfort food? Hungry Joe's and Bridgetown Roti will indulge you with dishes such as curried shrimp and oxtail or codfish cakes right here in the City of Angels. There is also Natraliart, in business for over three decades, which offers an extensive menu including juices, okra, and saltfish and ackee—the Jamaican national dish. The savory fruit and fish preparation is a staple and can be eaten any time of day. To get yourself around the city, hire a Rastabus to party Irie-style while you hit all the fun stops with reggae music playing loud.

Hungry Joe's jerk chicken is the second most popular dish on the menu.
Credit: Hungry Joe's

Japanese

The Garden of Water and Fragrance in San Fernando Valley. *Credit: The Japanese Garden*

Head to Little Tokyo for a visit to one of the most historic neighborhoods in Los Angeles. This is a National Historic Landmark offering everything from shopping plazas and anime stores to traditional and contemporary cuisine-focused restaurants. The Japanese American Cultural & Community Center campus here features LA native Isamu Noguchi's sculpture, *To the Issei.* The Japanese American National Museum campus includes a historic building that was previously the first Buddhist temple built in LA. Little Tokyo is also on the National Registry of Historic Places and designated a California Cultural District. Stop by the *Home Is Little Tokyo* mural to learn more about the history of the area, and if you stay at the Doubletree by Hilton in Downtown LA, then head to their Kyoto rooftop garden and pay attention to some of the interior details as well. The Geffen Contemporary at MOCA, an extension of MOCA on Grand Avenue, is here inside a former police-car warehouse. Shop at Bunkado, Sanrio or Marukai Market. A little further away in the heart of Hollywood is Japan House Los Angeles, which offers programming on Japanese culture, including design exhibitions, culinary events, and a serene library overlooking busy Hollywood Boulevard.

Food And Celebrations

Anime Expo
Azay
Café Dulce
Daikukoya
Donburi Cafe
Fugetsu-Do Bakery Shop
Gyu-KakuBBQ
Kabuki Restaurant
Katana
Katsuya
Los Angeles Asian Pacific Film Festival
Marugame Monzo
Men Oh Tokushima Ramen
n/naka
Nijiya Market
Nisei Week Festival
Nobu
Okoyama Kobo Bakery and Café
Oshogatsu Festival
Q Sushi
Sawtelle Japantown Celebration
Shunji Japanese Cuisine
Sugarfish by Sushi Nozawa
Sushi Gen
Takami Sushi and Robata
Yamashiro
Yabu Restaurant
World Market

Organizations And Institutions

East West Players
Go for Broke National Education Center and Monument
Hollywood Japanese Cultural Institute
Hompa Hongwanji Buddhist Temple
Japan House Los Angeles
Japanese American National Museum
Japanese Village Plaza
Kinokuniya Book Stores of America
Koyasan Beikoku Betsuin
Kudo Kai Archery Club
Little Tokyo Galleria
Senshin Buddhist Temple
The Garden of Water and Fragrance in San Fernando Valley
The Japan Foundation
The Japanese American Cultural & Community Center
Tuesday Night Project
Venice Japanese Community Center

Japanese: At Japan House Los Angeles, "Life Cycles" exhibition and bamboo artist Tanabe Chikuunsai IV. *Credit: Tadayuki Minamoto*

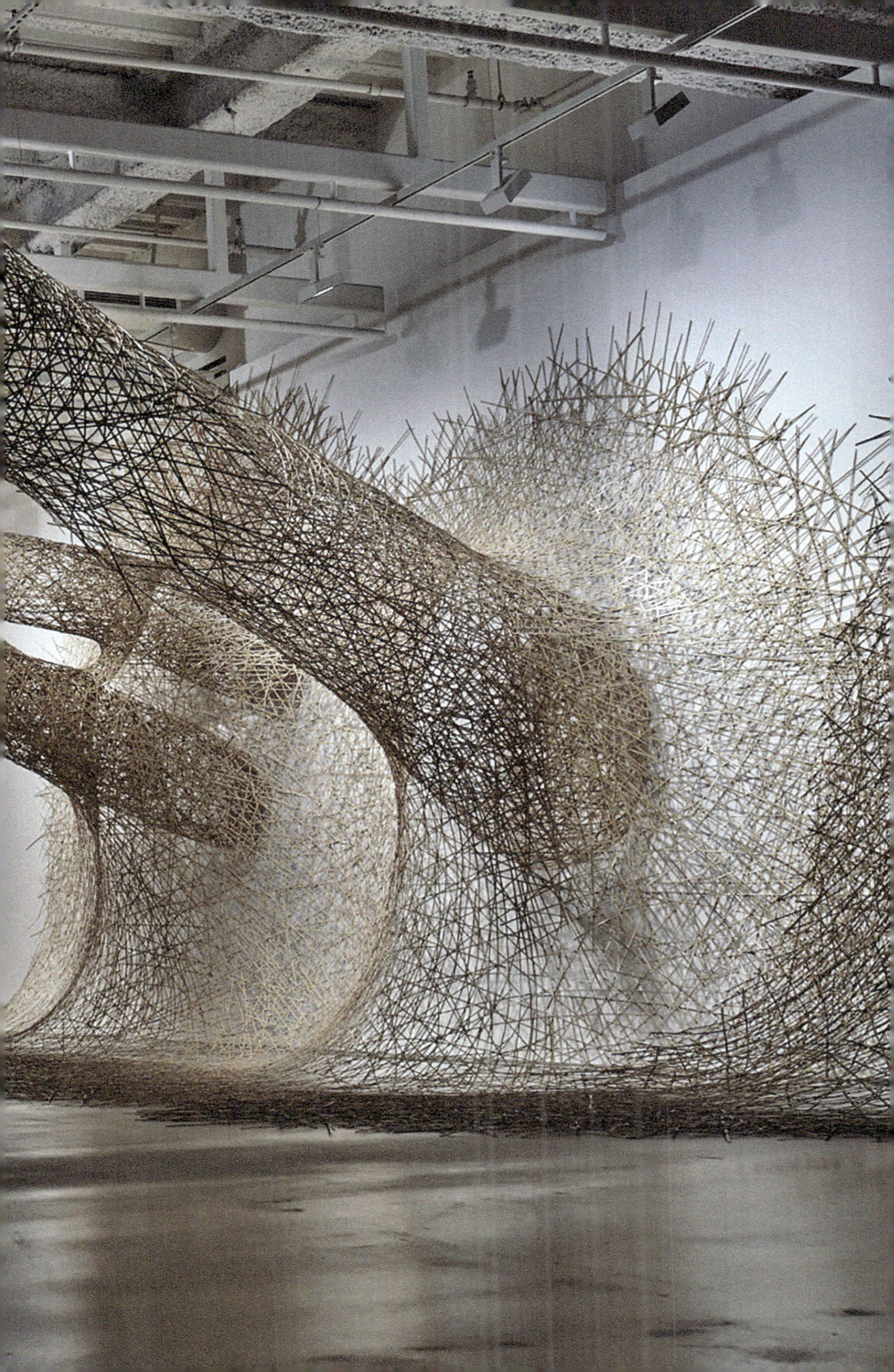

Food And Celebrations

Asian American and Pacific Islander Heritage Month in May

Dolan's Uyghur Cuisine

Eid and Ramadan celebrations

Era Grill halal food

EuroAsia Restaurant

Gleanoaks Kabab House

Gratitude Day celebrations

Independence Day celebrations

Kalinka Russian cuisine

Kashtan Restaurant and Deli

LA Chai Cart

Lazzat Grill

Los Angeles Asian Film Festival

Makkah Market

Mante House

Melad Bakery Restaurant and Catering

Nauryz spring celebrations

Navat Shawarma and Central Asian Food Truck

Saffron Food Mart

Shahi Mahal

Shor

Organizations And Institutions

California Qazaq Community

Islamic Center of Southern California

Kazakhs in Southern California Facebook group

King Fahad Mosque

Southern California Halal Foodies Instagram

University of California Los Angeles Asia Pacific Center Program on Central Asia

University of Southern California Los Angeles Department of Slavic, East European and Eurasian Languages and Cultures

West LA International Market

Kazakh

The Kazakh community is a small but active community in Los Angeles. Though they regularly gather for social events, there isn't a specific area of the county where they reside. The community meets for cultural celebrations such as the Nauryz new-year festival in the spring, which includes traditional dance and music performances, national-costume competitions, games, food, and a beauty pageant. The California Qazaq Community center hosts regular events and programming. There aren't community-specific eateries as such but some well-known Kazakhs reside in Los Angeles. Among them are the artists and performance duo Eldar Tagi and Lena Pozdnyakova (who go by "the2vvo"), and fashion maven Dina Kabdolla, known for her streetwear designs. Kabdolla is a strong player in the LA fashion scene, a multi-billion-dollar industry that doesn't typically see much Kazakh participation. Los Angeles hosts two fashion weeks a year—one in March and the other in October. Los Angeles Fashion Week is recognized by the Council of Fashion Designers of America, and recent editions have witnessed participation from designers such as Tadashi Shoji, known for his evening wear and red-carpet styles, and Simkhai, known for luxury ready-to-wear designs.

Plov with vegetables and meat is common at most Kazakh meals.
Credit: Ruksana Hussain

An assorted tray of Kazakh desserts.
Credit: Ruksana Hussain

Kenyan

Kahawa 1893's Kenyan coffee sourced from female farmers is sold in select Sprouts and Target store locations. *Credit: Kahawa 1893*

Given the diversity of the African population in Los Angeles, finding a variety of regional cuisines to savor across the city is no challenge. But why not attempt some recipes in your own kitchen, especially with a resource such as Kiano Moju's AfriCali: Recipes from my Jikoni cookbook to help with your efforts. Raised in California but born to a Kenyan mother and Nigerian father, Moju's recipe collection ensures your meals are a riot of flavor and fun as she brings together preparations inspired by her childhood and travels. Try your hand at some chapos (chapati) or mandazi (African donuts) to start but there is an entire book to journey through and lots to taste along the way so pace yourself. To accompany this culinary jaunt, sip on Kahawa 1893's small batch roasted Kenyan single origin coffee. The female-owned brand sources its specialty-grade beans directly from women farmers in Kenya and other African nations. Perhaps mandazi and coffee will prove apt companions as you watch the next Los Angeles Marathon, which Kenyans have won more frequently than runners from any other country over the course of the race's history. Talk about a flex, and a well-earned one at that.

Kiano Moju's recipes are a culinary adventure. *Credit: Kiano Moju*

Food And Celebrations

AfriCali Recipes from My Jikoni Cookbook

African Chop Food Truck

African Restaurant Week

Airport Royal Cuisine

Christmas celebrations

Dat Moi Market

Eid and Ramadan celebrations

Jamhuri Day celebrations

Kahawa 1893

Nkechi African Cafe

Nkwagala Cafe

Pan African Film and Arts Festival

Springbok Bar and Grill

Sumptuous African Restaurant

Sweet Jollof

The Eldo in Long Beach

The Peppered Goat

Toto's African Cuisine

Two Hommes

Ubuntu Vegan

Veronica's Kitchen

Vuuka restaurant

Weaf restaurant

Organizations And Institutions

African American Cultural Center

Consulate General of the Republic of Kenya

Ernie Wolfe Gallery

Fowler Museum at UCLA Mellon African Art Initiative

Kwanzaa Parade and Festival

Los Angeles County Museum of Art African Art Collection

Los Angeles Kenyans Facebook group

Rele Art Gallery

Southern California Kenyan Catholic Community

Zawadi Cultural Collective

Food And Celebrations

- AB Steak
- Angma Traditional Craft Brewing
- Big Bear Farm
- Bumsan Organic Milk Bar
- Chosun Galbee
- Daedo Sikdang
- DGM Soju Bar
- Genwa
- Hangari Kalguksu
- Jeong Yuk Jeom
- KCON LA
- Kobawoo House
- Koreatown Pizza Company
- LA Korean Festival
- LA Tofu House
- Lee Ga
- Mapo Chicken
- MDK Noodles
- Oakobing
- Paris Baguette
- Parks BBQ
- Prime K BBQ
- Quarters BBQ
- Shiku
- Soban
- Somi Somi Icecream
- Soowon Galbi
- Surawon Tofu House
- Ten-Raku
- Two Hands Fresh Corn Dogs

Organizations And Institutions

- 6ixth Sense
- Aroma Spa and Sports
- Brass Monkey
- California Market
- CGV Cinemas
- Chapman Market
- City Center on 6th
- Crystal Spa
- Da Wool Jung Pavilion Garden
- Garden Suite Hotel
- Gateway Sign
- K-Pop Music Town
- Korean American Musicians Association
- Korean Cultural Center
- Korean Friendship Bell
- Koreatown Galleria
- Koreatown Plaza
- LA Korean United Methodist Church
- Lee Wha Hanbok Dress Store
- Madang Mall
- Pharaoh Karaoke
- Rosen Karaoke
- Sejong Bookstore
- Seoul International Park
- Six Taste Tours
- The Venue
- Wi Spa

Korean

For a taste of Korea in LA, Koreatown or K-town is your destination. Easily accessed using the LA Metro, it's the spot for Korean food, shopping, entertainment—you name it! The area has become much more diverse over the years, with many other ethnicities also calling it home. K-town received official recognition in 1980 and is one of the densest neighborhoods in the country. A guided tour with LA Walking Tours might just be the key to finding your way around. Several famous Korean celebrities are from the Greater LA area including Chef Roy Choi of Kogi BBQ and Netflix's *The Chef Show* fame and Joshua Hong, member of Korean pop group Seventeen. With the rising popularity of K-pop, the KCON shows are a huge draw in LA.

Handmade mandu and hot pot at Lee Ga Korean Restaurant in Koreatown. *Credit: Lee Ga*

While you are in the neighborhood, stop by landmark locations such as The Wiltern, known for its Art Deco-style architecture, and the Normandie Club inside the historic Normandie Hotel—a stunning combination of Spanish colonial and Renaissance Revival design. The American Institute of Architects also hosts an architecture-themed tour in this area and the LA Conservancy has a self-guided tour option that is easy and fun.

Dine at Lee Ga Korean Restaurant for traditional Korean specialties. *Credit: Lee Ga*

Laotian

Lao Beef Larb with toasted rice powder and galangal. *Credit: Ruksana Hussain*

Within Los Angeles, dining is the primary Laotian experience one can expect given the small size of the population in the city proper. There are several restaurants that serve Laotian food so it is easy to get your fix of delicious papaya salad or larb (ground meat salad) and sticky rice. But finding other cultural experiences might not be as simple. To immerse yourself in the community here, connect with groups like Laos Angeles, which hosts regular meetings centered on networking, food, and other community member interests. The Laotian community is much more involved and culturally active in Orange County. But there are many celebrations for the Lao New Year in April and participating in the festivities is a wonderful way to experience the culture. There is also a large Hmong community in Long Beach and the group hosts events annually as well. The new-year celebrations include multiple musical and dance performances and are one of the best occasions to see the community don colorful traditional attire.

Lao Papaya Salad or Tam Mak Hoong is a crunchy, spicy delight. *Credit: Ruksana Hussain*

Food And Celebrations

- Aquarium of the Pacific Southeast Asia Day festival
- Boun Khoun Khao rice-harvest festival
- Cat Sengsourichanh | Baked Goods & Treats
- Hmong New Year celebrations
- Kim Thai Food
- Kop Jai Lai
- Lacha Somtum
- Lao National Day
- Lao New Year celebrations
- Los Angeles Asian Film Festival
- Los Angeles Asian Pacific Film Festival
- Malina Syvoravong Food and Beverage
- Now Serving
- Owl Owl Thai Lao Street Food
- Sabaidee Lao & Thai Street Food
- Saeng's Kitchen

Organizations And Institutions

- Hmong Association of Long Beach
- Laos Angeles Facebook group
- Los Angeles County Museum of Art South and Southeast Asian Art Collection
- Sayon Art
- TeAda Productions
- UCLA Center for Southeast Asian Studies

Food And Celebrations

Almaza

Ammatoli

Arab American Heritage Month celebrations in April

Big Al's Pizzeria

Bowery Bungalow

Café du Liban

Café X20

Carnival Restaurant

Carousel Restaurant

FurnSaj Bakery & Restaurant

Hayat's Kitchen

Jewish American Heritage Month celebrations in May

Jojo's Mediterranean Grill

Koko's

Ladyhawk

Levant Bistro

Mantee Café

Marouch

Mediterranean Bistro

Nazelie's Lebanese Cafe

Open Sesame Grill

Phoenicia

Pi on Sunset

RoRo's Chicken

Shawarma Street

Shawarma Time

Sumac Mediterranean

Sunnin Café

The Gate Lounge

X'Tiosu Oaxacan Arabesque Kitchen

Zahle Restaurant

Organizations And Institutions

Arab Market Venice Blvd

Cedars Meat Market

Consulate General of Lebanon

House of Lebanon Cultural Center

Lebanese in Los Angeles Facebook group

Lebanese Ladies Cultural Society

Los Angeles County Museum Art of the Middle East Collection

West LA International Market

Lebanese

The Lebanese community is part of the Arab population represented in California and, more specifically, in Los Angeles. There are Lebanese restaurants all over the city with some of the best hummus (chickpea dip), fattoush (salad with pita bread and greens), falafel (chickpea patties), kibbeh (ground meat and bulgur), and shawarma (meat wrapped in bread) to be found outside the Middle East. Bakeries and cafés serving baklava (phyllo dough pastry) and knafeh (sugary cheese pastry) as well as other dessert treats abound. Add in the hookah lounges for an extra dose of Lebanese culture and listen for the one with the loudest music and laughter. One essential dining spot is Ladyhawk at Hollywood hotel Kimpton La Peer where *Top Chef Middle East* season-five winner Charbel Hayek delves into his Lebanese roots to present family-style dining fare that has received rave reviews all over. To continue the theme, head to events by Beirut Nights Parties or Yalla Party Project LA, or a performance by Lebanese American artist Leila Milki.

Ammatoli in Long Beach makes sahlab, a Levantine milk drink flavored with orange blossom water.
Credit: Ammatoli

Koko's Middle Eastern restaurant's Maane, Arayes, and Bastrma.
Credit: Ruksana Hussain

Malaysian

Char Kway Teow is a popular dish in Singapore and Malaysia.
Credit: Mee and Greet

The Malaysian community in Los Angeles is not strongly represented in any one area despite its sizeable population. There are a handful of Malaysian restaurants in the city, the most notable of which is Chef Kenji Tang's Ipoh Kopitiam in Alhambra—a fantastic spot should you choose to dine there. Whether you crave toast with kaya (coconut jam), roti canai (flatbread) with curry, nasi lemak (rice cooked in coconut milk and pandan leaf), or asam laksa (fish-based rice-noodle soup), you are guaranteed to find that and more at this Michelin Bib Gourmand–rated eatery.

For other community events in LA, the Malaysian Association of Southern California has an event calendar you can consult as you make your plans. Most other restaurants present a variety of cuisines with a few Malaysian options or have Asian fusion cuisine, which incorporates Malaysian-inspired dishes. Fusion food is prevalent in LA and sometimes includes the most unexpected combinations imaginable, making for an interesting dining experience. Think Peruvian pasta, Korean pizza, Indian poutine … you get the idea. With the melting pot of cultures that is LA, there are bound to be the melding of cuisines as well. Fortunately, there are many chefs in the city who do it gloriously.

Food And Celebrations

Aquarium of the Pacific Southeast Asia Day festival

Asian American and Pacific Islander Heritage Month in May

Bone Kettle Restaurant

Diwali celebrations

Eid and Ramadan celebrations

Family Halal Meat Market

Fragrant Jerky

Ipoh Kopitiam

Gleanoaks Kabab House

Halal Kitchen Café

LA Chai Cart

Los Angeles Asian Film Festival

Mee and Greet

Melad Bakery Restaurant and Catering

Mutiara Halal Food and Market

Saffron Food Mart

Sam Tan's Kitchen

Shor

Skewers Halal

West LA International Market

Organizations And Institutions

Club Singaporean-Americans LA/OC

Consulate General of Malaysia

Islamic Center of San Gabriel Valley

Los Angeles County Museum of Art South and Southeast Asian Art Collection

Malaysian Association of Southern California

Malaysian Food Lovers LA

Malaysian Islamic Foundation of North America

UCLA Center for Southeast Asian Studies

Food And Celebrations

Bar Hermanito
Birrieria de Don Boni
Café Calle
Casa Vega
Casita del Campo
Cielito Lindo
Damian
Día de los Muertos
East LA Mexican
El Paseo Inn
Fiesta Broadway Cinco de Mayo
Gish Bac
Gracias Madre
Guelaguetza
Holbox
Independence Day Parade and Festival
Joselito's
LA Cha Cha Cha
Los Angeles Latino International Film Festival
Mexican American Film and Television Festival & Awards
National Hispanic Heritage Month
Night of the Blaxican
Rodeo Mexican Grill
Sad Girl Creamery
Sara's Market

Organizations And Institutions

Avenue 50 Studio
Avila Adobe
Bermudez Projects
Bilingual Foundation of the Arts
Cactus Gallery
El Mercado de Los Angeles
El Pueblo de Los Angeles Historical Monument
La Galeria Rebelde
La Placita Church
La Plaza de Cultura y Artes
Latino Outdoors
Latino Theater Company
Mexican Center for Culture and Cinematic Arts
Mexican Cultural Institute
Paseo de La Plaza
Pico House
Plaza de La Raza
Plaza Park
The Great Wall of Los Angeles
The Mistake Room

Mexican

Start at Olvera Street—along the LA Marathon route—where you can experience the oldest parts of Los Angeles and learn about some of the historic structures. Visit during celebrations such as Día de los Reyes, Fiesta de la Candelaria, or Las Posadas to see the area in festive mode. Then take Cesar Chavez Avenue toward Boyle Heights where a notable Mexican American population resides, though it isn't the only representation within the LA city area. You'll find many murals and shops here. Head to the Natural History Museum for the *Sin Censura* mural now displayed in its permanent home. Find more murals to visit on the Mural Conservancy of LA database online. The Universal City metro station also features murals related to Mexican history. In fact, you can enjoy art at every metro train station—look up the LA Metro art website for artwork by location or artist. If pressed for time, then the East LA Latin Flavors tour with Melting Pot Tours is a splendid option. If not, then a short drive away in Long Beach is Museum of Latin American Art, the only museum in the country showcasing modern and contemporary Latin American and Latino art.

Casita del Campo's lively interiors and delicious Mexican food. *Credit: Three Fold Agency*

LA Cha Cha Cha serves tacos and cocktails in a stylish rooftop setting. *Credit: LA Cha Cha Chá*

Moroccan

Moun of Tunis specializes in Moroccan cuisine in Los Angeles. *Credit: Ruksana Hussain*

Los Angeles has a large Moroccan population, most of which has settled in the Pico-Robertson, North Hollywood, and Beverly Hills areas over the years. A sizeable Moroccan Jewish community lives in LA as well. Finding a spot to enjoy some Moroccan flavors isn't a challenge—there are some venues that specialize in the cuisine and others that have Mediterranean and halal options. Tagine Beverly Hills by Chef Ben Benameur is a hidden little gem of a dining experience where you can choose from seafood bastilla (savory pie), zaalouk (eggplant and tomato salad), and a variety of tagine (stew) and couscous preparations. Not so hidden is the fact that the restaurant is also owned by actor Ryan Gosling, adding to the list of Los Angeles culinary establishments with Hollywood celebrity interest.

Other restaurants that have similar star investment include Hilltop Coffee + Kitchen (Issa Rae), Crossroads Kitchen (Travis Barker), and Casita (Anderson Paak). And while there is no official map of celebrity-owned venues, a new list pops up every now and then reminding you that there is a faint possibility a celebrity owner may happen to visit their restaurant the day you dine there.

Food And Celebrations

Ammatoli

Arab American Heritage Month celebrations in April

Barsha restaurant

Bavel

Bowery Bungalow

Café Landwer

Carnival Restaurant

Casablanca Moroccan Kitchens

Chef Yasmina's cooking class

Crimson restaurant

Elf Café

Glendale Shawarma

Jewish American Heritage Month celebrations in May

Kismet

Marsa Mediterranean

Mazal restaurant

Mizlala Mediterranean

Momed restaurant

Moun of Tunis Restaurant

Pan African Film and Arts Festival

Saffy's restaurant

Salam Falafel

Samos Café and Grill

Sebastian's Mediterranean

Tagine Beverly Hills

Organizations And Institutions

Badia Design Authentic Moroccan Furniture

Ernie Wolfe Gallery

Fowler Museum at UCLA Mellon African Art Initiative

Kantara Rugs

Los Angeles County Museum of Art African Art Collection

Mehraban Rugs

Moroccan American Community in Los Angeles Facebook group

Moroccans in Los Angeles Facebook group

Mosaik Furniture and Décor

Rele Art Gallery

University of California Los Angeles Moroccan Jewish Studies

University of California Los Angeles Sephardic Archive Initiative

Food And Celebrations

American Indian Community Council Christmas Toy Drive

American Indian Festival at The Autry Museum of the American West

Aquarium of the Pacific Moompetam American Indian Festival

Indigenous Peoples Day

Indigenous Pride LA

LA Skinsfest Film Festival

Lucy Hale's Indian Tacos and Frybread

Malibu Chumash Day Native American Powwow and Intertribal Gathering

Native American Heritage Month celebrations in November

NFMLA Monthly Film Festival | InFocus: Indigenous Cinema

Organizations And Institutions

American Indian Community Council

Antelope Valley Indian Museum State Historic Park

Autry Museum of the American West

Catalina Museum for Art and History

Chumash Indian Museum

Fowler Museum at UCLA Pimu Catalina Island Archaeology Project

Gabrieleno San Gabriel Band of Mission Indians Gabrieleno-Tongva Nation

Haramokngna American Indian Cultural Center

Kuruvungna Springs Village Cultural Center

Natural History Museum

Rancho Los Cerritos

The Museum of the San Fernando Valley

United American Indian Involvement Inc.

Wishtoyo Chumash Village

Native American

The Gabrieleño/Tongva Nation, the aboriginal tribe of the Los Angeles Basin, were the first Angelenos. There are three tribes in Los Angeles County that are recognized by the state—the Ventureño, Gabrieleño-Tongva, and Fernandeño. In fact, the heart of the Los Angeles County Seal features a Tongva woman. And now you know where Santa Monica's Tongva Park gets its name. Another public spot where you can see the tribe honored is at the Electric Fountain in Beverly Gardens Park at the corner of Santa Monica and Wilshire Boulevards. Glance up and you will notice a statue of a Tongva-Gabrieleño Native American tribal member kneeling in prayer. The beautiful public art sculpture is lit up at night and quite the local star at a busy intersection. There are several other public works across the county honoring the first Angelenos. But if you only have time for one event then an intertribal gathering or powwow is a must for learning more about the Native American community and supporting them as they honor their legacy. Online, the exhibit in the Autry Museum of the American West, When I Remember, I See Red, is a powerful resource to view anytime.

The Autry Museum of the American West showcases Native American life. *Credit: Autry Museum of the American West*

The Chumash Indian Museum is a Native American Interpretive Center in Thousand Oaks. *Credit: Chumash Indian Museum*

Nepali

A hearty, flavorful thukpa is a guaranteed dish on any Nepali restaurant's menu. *Credit: Ruksana Hussain*

Los Angeles is home to a large Nepali population that supports several restaurants in the city. However, as a community, they're not as visible as their South Asian counterparts, which makes pinpointing a neighborhood where the culture can be experienced a bit challenging. That said, every now and then you might chance upon a cluster of businesses together, in Pasadena or Santa Monica, and if you are in luck, you can find a restaurant that has Nepali momo (steamed dumplings wth a variety of fillings) and thukpa (noodle soup) on their menu. In addition, some Indian restaurants serve their own versions of momo, which are quite good. The few Nepali dining establishments that are well-known are dispersed throughout the city so dining at a Nepali venue must sometimes be a destination trip. If you see a Himalayan Café or Himalayan House pop up as you travel around Los Angeles, do yourself a favor and stop by. For a little retail therapy, Kathmandu Boutique and Himalaya Handmade have clothing, accessories and other products from Nepal.

Nepali momo is filled with seasoned meat or vegetables. *Credit: Ruksana Hussain*

Food And Celebrations

23rd Street Café

Arth Culver City

Asian American and Pacific Islander Heritage Month in May

Baar Baar LA

Cinnamon Indian cuisine

Dashain celebrations

Diwali and Holi celebrations

Himalayan Café

Himalayan House restaurant

House of Curry

Indian Film Festival of Los Angeles

Kamal Palace

Los Angeles Asian Film Festival

Los Angeles Asian Pacific Film Festival

Mayura

Momo Fomo

Mr. Masala

Nanking Artesia

Shor

Tara's Himalayan Cuisine

Tibet Nepal House restaurant

Tulsi Eatery

Organizations And Institutions

Bhagavad-Gita Museum

Himalaya Handmade

Hindu Temple and Cultural Center

International Society for Krishna Consciousness

Kathmandu Boutique

Los Angeles Gurung Society (Tamu Samaj)

Los Angeles Nepalese Community

Nepali Community Center

Shree Pashupatinath Foundation, USA

Southern California Nepali Entertainment Network

Southern California Nepali Society Facebook group

The Norton Simon Museum South and Southeast Asian Collections

United Nepalese in Los Angeles Facebook group

Food And Celebrations

Aquarium of the Pacific Noche de Estrellas

Café de Leche

Café Integral at Freehand Hotel

Central American Festival and Parade

El Camacho Restaurante Nicaraguense

Garifuna International Indigenous Film Festival

Garifuna Settlement Day Mass

La 27th Restaurante

La Adelita restaurant

La Ceiba restaurant

La Fritanga

Las Segovias restaurant

Museum of Latin American Art Afro-Latinx Festival

National Hispanic Heritage Month

Picaresca Barra De Cafe & Casa Tostadora

Portobanco's restaurant

Restaurante Managua

Reyes Coffee

Sabor Nicaraguense restaurant

Organizations And Institutions

Bilingual Foundation of the Arts

Central American Confederation

Garifuna American Heritage Foundation United

Garifuna Museum of LA

Heart of Samba Entertainment

Museum of Latin American Art

The Broad

Nicaraguan

Belizean punta rock artist Bootsy Ranking at an interview at the Garifuna Museum. *Credit: Media Marathon*

While many other countries have adopted it as their own, historians agree that we have Nicaragua to thank for the marvel that is a tres-leches cake. Thankfully, there are several Nicaraguan restaurants in Los Angeles where you can find not just the tres-leches cake but also traditional Nicaraguan cuisine. Some of the venues have extensive menus and will require multiple visits to do justice to the meal. LA, in fact, has quite the love affair with desserts. There are pastry shops, cafés, and bakeries all around, with choices from the classics to the most innovative concoctions and ingredients when it comes to sweet treats. Especially if the menu is seasonal, and featuring fresh local California produce, chances are you will be returning for more.

Take a break from the culinary for the cultural and head to the Museum of Latin American Art or the Garifuna Museum if wandering the city is part of the agenda or plan to attend the Central American Festival and Parade.

At the Garifuna Museum, pictures of Garinagu women selling coconuts. *Credit: Media Marathon*

Nigerian

At ILÉ Private Dining Room, Chef Eros presents Dambu-Nama, dried beef floss. *Credit: ILÉ Private Dining Room*

Nigerian actors who have called Los Angeles home include celebrities like Chiwetel Ejiofor and David Oyelowo. However, in the local landscape, the real celebrities are the small businesses and Nigerian chefs slowly but surely taking over the city with their tantalizing flavors and aromas. With spices and other ingredients unique to each country in West Africa, the Nigerian community stands out largely due to the number of members living in areas like Inglewood, Compton, and other parts of South Los Angeles. Chef Eros of ILÉ Home has made quite a splash with his seven-course private dining experiences that are culinary journeys as well as educational revelations for those trying West African cuisine for the first time. Invitations to his catering events at large outdoor venues such as Coachella are coveted by all. Several other eateries across Los Angeles County offer jollof rice, egusi soup (made with egusi melon seeds), dodo (fried plantain), and other traditional dishes, and that usually includes some rhythmic Nigerian Afrobeats playing in the background providing a worthy pairing with an exceptional meal. Dig into some fufu (cassava dish) and stew while you ponder the ongoing debate—who makes the best jollof rice?

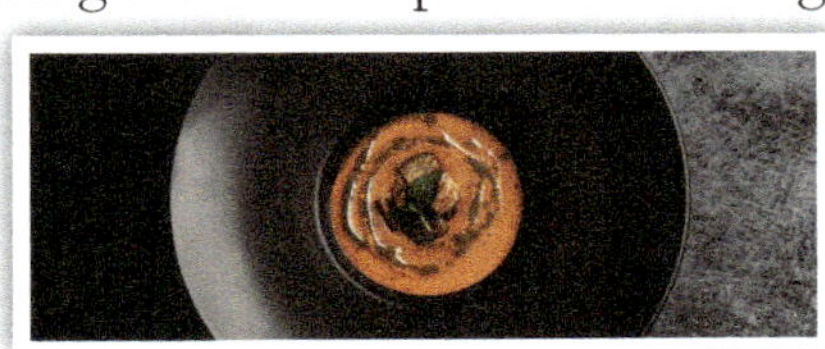

Chef Eros' Nigerian butternut squash soup served at ILÉ Private Dining Room. *Credit: ILÉ Private Dining Room*

Food And Celebrations

Aduke Cuisine and Lounge

AfriCali Recipes from My Jikoni Cookbook

African Chop Food Truck

African Obichi Food Store

African Restaurant Week

AfroBeat Los Angeles

Alta West African

Dat Moi Market

Èkó Kitchen Modern Nigerian Cooking

ILÉ Private Dining Room

Kwanzaa Parade and Festival

Minaco Ventures African Food Market

Nkechi African Cafe

Nkwagala Café

Pan African Film and Arts Festival

Sumptuous African Restaurant

Sweet Jollof

The Peppered Goat

Ubuntu Vegan

Veronica's Kitchen

Weaf restaurant

Organizations And Institutions

African American Cultural Center

Art + Practice

California African American Museum

Dembrebrah West African Drum & Dance Ensemble

Ernie Wolfe Gallery

Fowler Museum at UCLA Mellon African Art Initiative

Inner City Cultural Center

Los Angeles County Museum of Art African Art Collection

Lula Washington Dance Theater

Malik Books

Nigerians in Southern California Facebook group

Rele Art Gallery

The Broad

The National Association of African American Parents & Youth

The William Grant Still Arts Center

Zawadi Cultural Collective

Nigerian: ILÉ Private Dining Room is an intimate dining experience. *Credit: ILÉ Private Dining Room*

Food And Celebrations

Al Noor

Al Watan

Asian American and Pacific Islander Heritage Month in May

Biriyani Kabob House

Chargha House

Eid and Ramadan celebrations

Family Halal Meat Market

Famous Tandoori

Gleanoaks Kabab House

Halal Kabob House

Halal Kitchen Café

Independence Day celebrations

Kausar Halal Meat Market

LA Chai Cart

Makkah Market

Now Serving

Saffron Food Mart

Shahi Mahal

SHOR

Skewers Halal

Tawakal Halal Tandoori restaurant

West LA International Market

Zam Zam Foods

Organizations And Institutions

Artesia City Church

Consulate General of Pakistan

Hindi Urdu United Methodist Mission Congregation

Islamic Center of Southern California

King Fahad Mosque

Pakistani American Arts Council

Pakistani American Chamber of Commerce

Pakistanis in Los Angeles Facebook group

Southern California Cricket Association

The Norton Simon Museum South and Southeast Asian Painting and Sculpture Collection

University of Southern California Pacific Asia Museum Pakistan Arts Council

Pakistani

Most of the Pakistani population in Los Angeles reside in Little India or Artesia. It is also called the International Cultural and Shopping District as people from several other cultural communities also live here but it is still known unofficially as Little India. There are many restaurants and grocery stores here but there are also clothing shops selling outfits such as traditional shalwar kameez, kurtas, and suits, for both men and women, so this is a great spot to head to when you receive a last-minute invitation to a South Asian wedding. Most families head here to get multiple things accomplished, often dining out after stocking up on groceries. Enjoy cooking South Asian dishes at home? Visit Little India for the right herbs, spices, and curries. Little Arabia in Orange County is also just a few minutes away so that's a bonus if you plan your visit right.

The food spread at SHOR is a culmination of cuisines from Afghanistan, India, and Pakistan. *Credit: Andrew Bui*

A custom chai cart serving delicious chai from LA Chai Cart. *Credit: Amber Rain Photography*

Peruvian

Professional Peruvian folk artist Nadia Calmet specializes in Afro-Peruvian dances.
Credit: Enzo Amado

Afro Peruvian Culture Day in Los Angeles spotlights the performing arts to educate visitors about the cultural diversity of Peru with food, dance, theater, and art. Founder Nadia Calmet is a professional Peruvian folk artist who specializes in Afro-Peruvian dancing, which she performs and teaches in LA. Check online to see how you can access her sessions.

There are other opportunities for music and dance experiences across LA that offer similar cultural significance. It is easy to review listings online for theater performances across multiple locations to find a show during your time in the city. Many such performances are held in classic venues that have historic as well as aesthetic value. Sometimes you can also tour the venue itself but may have to request in advance, schedule an appointment with on-site staff, or obtain a timed entry ticket so remember to visit the venue's website before you make your way there to ensure you've got those arrangements organized.

Mee and Greet's Bo Luc Lac Saltado is a Peruvian classic with Vietnamese flair.
Credit: Mee and Greet

Food And Celebrations

- Aquarium of the Pacific Noche de Estrellas
- Cabra restaurant
- Catalina's Market
- Chios Peruvian Grill
- Con Sabor a Peru
- Dat Moi Market
- Don Felix Fine Peruvian Cuisine
- El Pollon on the Road
- Inca Market at Peru Village
- Inka Wasi
- Llama Love Vegan
- Los Angeles Latino International Film Festival
- Los Balcones
- Mariscos 4 Vientos
- Mercado La Paloma
- Mex Peru Gipsy
- Mikhuna Food Truck
- Natalie Peruvian Seafood Restaurant
- Pisco Sour Market
- Puro Sabor

Organizations And Institutions

- Afro Peruvian Experience Performing Arts Company
- Bilingual Foundation of the Arts
- Heart of Samba Entertainment
- Peru Village
- Raices Peruana Cultural Dance Group
- The Broad
- Vincent Price Art Museum

Food And Celebrations

Celebration of Hannukah: Festival of Lights in December

Christmas celebrations

Dozynki harvest festival

EuroAsia Restaurant

European Deli Market

Krakow Ball

Mechta International Deli

Mom, Please Ukrainian Food

Otto's European and Hungarian Import Store & Deli

Pacific Coast Food

Pierogi Cooking Class

Polish American Heritage Month celebrations in October

Polish Day in LA

Polish Festival Los Angeles

Polish Film Festival

Polka Restaurant

Schreiner's Fine Sausages

Solidarity Restaurant

Strada Eateria and Bar

West LA International Market

Organizations And Institutions

Consulate General of the Republic of Poland

Holocaust Museum Los Angeles

Jewish Federation Los Angeles

Los Angeles County Museum of Art European Painting and Sculpture Collection

Los Angeles Public Library International Languages Department

Our Lady of the Bright Mount Church

Polish American Congress of Southern California

Polish Center in Los Angeles

Skirball Cultural Center

USC Thornton School of Music Polish Music Center

Wende Museum

Polish

Polish cultural celebrations are held annually during harvest season along with other festivities during heritage month when there is plenty of borscht, pierogis, and vodka to enjoy. There is also a Polish film festival that honors Polish filmmakers, young talent, and Polish characters portrayed in films. In addition, Los Angeles has an interesting arts connection to Poland with artist and sculptor Stanislav Szukalski who was a resident of Burbank until his death in the 1980s. Actor Leonardo DiCaprio became interested in Szukalski's work and has since made a biographical documentary featuring the artist called *Struggle*. Although not currently featured in any local museums in LA, the film is expected to increase interest in the sculptor so that more of his work will become accessible. More recently though, Polish artists have exhibited at several galleries and museums in the city. Arts play a big role in Los Angeles and not a week goes by that some arts event, festival, show, or other related experience is happening in town. Neighborhoods host their own art shows too so mark your calendars for art walks in Downtown, Leimert Park, Culver City, Frogtown, and El Segundo.

Outdoor art and interactive artwork at the El Segundo ArtWalk. *Credit: City of El Segundo*

Mom Please Ukrainian Food's home-style pelmeni dumplings. *Credit: Mom Please Ukrainian Café*

Puerto Rican

Avenue 50 Studio is an arts presentation organization grounded in Latina/o culture and visual arts. *Credit: Avenue 50 Studio*

If you are near Los Angeles in June, make your way to Long Beach for the Puerto Rican Festival of Southern California—Día de los Muertos de San Juan. It is not the only Puerto Rican festival, but it is one of the best known. The large Puerto Rican presence in the city is a pleasant surprise and you can't go very far without noticing homes flying the Puerto Rican flag out on the patio or little eating spots advertising homemade mofongo (popular dish made with mashed fried green plantains). That blending of cultures over the centuries has resulted in comida criolla or creole food, which is what traditional Puerto Rican cuisine is called.

Puerto Rican artists also incorporate that fusion of cultures into their work and you can view their sculptures and artworks across the city in museums and public spaces. Lena del Sol specializes in Puerto Rican art and décor and her work can be seen across parts of North Hollywood, where she has painted several utility boxes and even a mural on a wall outside Mofongos Comida Criolla. This popular restaurant has been cooking Taino, Spanish, and African delicacies since 2009—oh, and bring your dancing shoes when you go.

Food And Celebrations

Casa Cabo Rojo

Dat Moi Market

Día de los Muertos at Olvera Street

Dia de San Juan Festival

El Nuevo Mundo Market

Forest Lawn Día de los Muertos celebrations

Hollywood Forever Día de los Muertos celebrations

House of Empanadas

Inglewood Hispanic Heritage Festival

La Casa de Iris

Los Muertos 5k run

Mofongos Comida Criolla

National Hispanic Heritage Month

Now Serving

Tainos LA restaurant

Taller Kurubina: Bomba in LA

Organizations And Institutions

Avenue 50 Studio

Bilingual Foundation of the Arts

Dominguez Rancho Adobe Museum

El Monte Historical Museum

El Sereno Community Arts Foundation

Gloria Molina Grand Park

Latino Theater Company

Mission Playhouse Día de los Muertos

Museum of Latin American Art

Music Center

Olvera Street Merchants Association

Pico Rivera Historical Museum

Plenazo Tribe Band

The Broad

Vincent Price Art Museum

Food And Celebrations

A-1 Imported Groceries Italian Market & Deli

Antoanela's Bakery

European Deli Market

Aroma Cafe

Black Jack Market

Divino

Kiff Kafe

Metro Cafe

Mignon Wine Bar

Monta Factory

Now Serving

Otto's European and Hungarian Import Store & Deli

Pacific Coast Food

Pirozzi's Italian Deli

Romanian National Day

San Pedro Cafe

Schreiner's Fine Sausages

Sebastian's Mediterranean

South East European Film Festival

South Shores Meat San Pedro

Strada Eateria and Bar

Sweets A LA-Cluj

Organizations And Institutions

Blind Lizard Balkan Band

Consulate General of Romania in Los Angeles

Holy Trinity Romanian American Orthodox Church

Los Angeles County Museum of Art European Painting and Sculpture Collection

Romani in Los Angeles

Viitorul Roman Cultural and Aid Society

Romanian

The Romanian community has been well represented in Hollywood. You have probably seen their work and not realized how many celebrities there are. The list of actors and/or singers includes Dustin Hoffman, Lauren Bacall, Art Garfunkel, Sebastian Stan, and Fran Drescher, who all have Romanian heritage. The Romanian American population in Los Angeles is extremely active and hosts programming all year long for community members. Particularly exciting is the South East European Film Festival, which exposes movie lovers to international talent and showcases an inclusive range of works from across Europe by covering more than 20 countries. Programming includes a theater schedule and virtual festival, and several music, arts, and related events before and after the film fest as well. Film categories include animation, documentary, experimental, feature, short, and more. LA's love affair with the movies is no secret—this is but one more avenue to explore global cinema right at our doorstep, in addition to all of the existing film fests already in LA. How lucky are we?

Grab this classic Romanian ROM chocolate bar at gourmet grocery stores. *Credit: Ruksana Hussain*

Romanian palinca is best served chilled with light appetizers. *Credit: Ruksana Hussain*

Russian

The City of West Hollywood's Annual WeHo Mishka Cultural Festival celebrates the Russian-speaking community. *Credit: City of West Hollywood | Alec Wolvec*

A large Russian-speaking population resides in the West Hollywood area of Los Angeles, making it the hub of celebration and activities for the community. Take a walk here during the day by the community center in Plummer Park and you will hear Russian conversation all around. The City of West Hollywood hosts several events throughout the year and the office houses a Russian-language public library. In fact, several Los Angeles Public Library branches in and around the area have dedicated Russian-language sections and host free programming such as talks, performances, movie screenings, and more.

The annual WeHo Mishka Festival and associated events attract possibly the largest gathering and celebration of the community in the greater Los Angeles area. Several Russian-owned businesses are sprinkled along the streets here but Traktir, a restaurant just a few minutes away from Plummer Park, offers dumplings such as vareniki and pelmeni, and other Eastern European favorites. On weekends, use WeHo's free ride service trolley called the PickUp so you don't have to worry about finding parking. Routes and times are published online for easy navigation around the neighborhood.

Food And Celebrations

Anniversary of Victory in Europe Day

Candyland Show

Caviar and Delicatessen Russian-Armenian Deli & Grocery

Celebration of Hannukah: Festival of Lights in December

Colibri Dance Festival

Colibri Vocal Competition

EuroAsia Restaurant

Kashtan Restaurant and Deli

MaySky Classical Night

Mechta International Deli

Mishka Arts and Culture Week Festival

Pacific Coast Food

Robert's Russian Cuisine

Tashkent Produce

Traktir

Weho Russian-speaking Community Cultural Heritage Month celebrations

West LA International Market

Organizations And Institutions

Getty Villa Museum

Holy Virgin Mary Russian Orthodox Cathedral

Los Angeles County Museum of Art

Marat Daukayev Ballet School

Plummer Park Monument

Showtime Katusha Dance Studio

The Broad

The Museum of Jurassic Technology Dogs of the Soviet

Space Program Collection

Wende Museum

Food And Celebrations

Amalia's

Aquarium of the Pacific Noche de Estrellas

Arroz and Fun

Café La Praviana

Central American Festival and Parade

Cipota Coffee

El Carrusel Bakery

El Día del Salvadoreño

El Mercadito Salvadoreño

Feria Agostina Celebration

Jaragua Copper Still

Kailey's

La Original Panaderia El Salvador

La Pupusa Urbana

Los Molcajetes

Mama's International Tamales

Mis Raices

National Hispanic Heritage Month

Restaurante Salvadoreño

Salvadoran Independence Day Parade

Salvi Fest

Sarita's Pupuseria at Grand Central Market

Organizations And Institutions

Avenue 50 Studio

Bilingual Foundation of the Arts

Central American Confederation

Consulate General of El Salvador

LaPau Gallery

Latino Outdoors

Latino Theater Company

Los Angeles County Museum of Art's Art of the Ancient Americas and Latin American Art

Museum of Latin American Art

Salvi Soul Food Culture and Community

The Association of Salvadorans of Los Angeles

The Broad

The Floricanto Center for the Performing Arts

Translatina Coalition

Viver Brasil Dance Company

Salvadoran

The only official recognition of the Salvadoran population in the United States is the El Salvador Community Corridor off the Union Station Metro stop south of downtown LA. Similar to a huge market, here you will find great deals from hundreds of street vendors selling food, fashion, household goods, and more. It extends on both sides of the Santa Monica Freeway so don't miss out on any part of it. Relish Salvadoran delicacies such as pupusas (stuffed corn tortillas), quesadilla (made from rice flour), and tamales (corn dough mixture with fillings wrapped and cooked in corn husk or banana leaves) along the way or, better yet, follow Salvi Soul on Instagram for ideas on the local dining scene. Not too far from here is the Original Los Angeles Flower Market as well as the Piñata District where you can find piñatas for every occasion. The Velaslavasay Panorama is near here as well, but it is only viewable by appointment so plan ahead. It is a 360-degree painted panorama housed inside the historic Union Theatre—an interesting way to experience what life was like before moving pictures and sound came along.

Hard to miss Kailey's Salvadoran housed in a bright yellow building. *Credit: Ruksana Hussain*

El Carrusel Bakery's Salvadoran, Mexican, and Guatemalan pastries. *Credit: Ruksana Hussain*

Singaporean

Mee and Greet's Hainan Chicken Rice is a Singaporean national dish. *Credit: Mee and Greet*

The best places to find Singaporean cuisine in Los Angeles are at Litz in Monterey Park or at Banana Leaf, inside the Original Farmers Market—the Singapore-style rice/noodle dishes are fabulous at both. Several other restaurants such as Mee and Greet present pan-Asian cuisine with some Singaporean dishes, but not many places sell a well-crafted Singapore Sling and you won't find anything similar to the hawker stalls in Singapore itself. That said, the Farmers Market is a great location for experiencing other cuisines and for enjoying what many consider a quintessential Los Angeles experience—open-air or outdoor malls. The Grove is one such location. In downtown, The Bloc and Fig@7th, Santa Monica Place with the Promenade, Westfield Century City Plaza, and even the closest outlet malls (quite the shopper's paradise if that's a new-to-you concept) all offer the indoor-outdoor mall experience. You can also try food halls for a variety of cuisines. Grand Central Market, Corporation Food Hall, Citizen Public Market, and Taste Food Hall are just a few such food halls where multiple dining choices are available within one venue—perfect for larger groups where everyone can find dishes suited to their tastes and preferences.

The Grove Tree Lighting Ceremony attracts large crowds. *Credit: Tiffany Rose*

Food And Celebrations

- Aquarium of the Pacific Celebration of Asian Culture Autumn Festival
- Aquarium of the Pacific Southeast Asia Day Festival
- Asia Supermarket
- Asian American and Pacific Islander Heritage Month in May
- Awan Dessert Shop
- Blasteran Beverly Hills
- Bone Kettle Restaurant
- Cassia restaurant
- Christmas celebrations
- Cluck2Go Hainan Chicken
- Diwali celebrations
- East Hollywood Farmers Market
- Eid and Ramadan celebrations
- Mae Malai House of Noodles
- Mee and Greet
- Night & Market
- Noodle Stars
- Plus62 Street Food
- Prata House
- Singapore's Banana Leaf

Organizations And Institutions

- Club Singaporean-Americans LA/OC
- Hsi Lai Temple
- Islamic Center of Southern California
- Los Angeles County Library Asian Pacific Resource Center
- Los Angeles County Museum of Art South and Southeast Asian Art Collection
- The Norton Simon Museum South and Southeast Asian Painting and Sculpture
- University of Southern California Pacific Asia Museum
- USC Fisher Museum of Art
- West LA International Market

Singaporean: Mee and Greet's Lunar New Year spread is a Pan Asian bonanza. *Credit: Mee and Greet*

Food And Celebrations

Africa Day celebrations

African Obichi Food Store

African Restaurant Week

Alta Adams Restaurant

Blume and Plume Coffee

Bohemian House of Espresso+Chai

Champignon Eats

Eldo Bar and Grill

European Deluxe Sausage Kitchen Beverly Hills

Kwanzaa Parade and Festival

Pan African Film and Arts Festival

Prosperity Market at the Natural History Museum

Rose Gold Pastries

South LA Cafe

Springbok Bar and Grill

Stellies Wines

Toto's African Cuisine

Organizations And Institutions

African American Cultural Center

Art + Practice

California African American Museum

Ernie Wolfe Gallery

Fowler Museum at UCLA Mellon African Art Initiative

Inner City Cultural Center

Los Angeles County Museum of Art African Art Collection

Malik Books

Rele Art Gallery

Reparations Club

South African Consulate General in Los Angeles

Southern Guild Art Gallery

The William Grant Still Arts Center

UCLA African Studies Center

Zawadi Cultural Collective

South African

Durban curry and biltong (cured meat snack) aren't the easiest foods to find in sunny Southern California, but the Eldo in Long Beach and the Springbok Bar and Grill—which serves Boerewors Rolls (made with spiced meat sausages) along with its curry—will make it happen. Nothing less than a South African wine will do to accompany the meal so Stellies Wines presents some of South Africa's best Stellenbosch pours to get the party going. While Stellies specializes in South African wines, finding other specialty wines in Los Angeles can be a thrill. Gourmet Wine and Spirits and Mel&Rose are two venues with impressive wine varietals. But in California, there are many wine festivals available for those whose leisurely pursuits include sipping fine wine. The choices include the LA Wine and Food Festival, Uncorked LA Wine Fest, Rosé Day LA, Garagiste Wine Festival, and the San Fernando Valley Food and Wine Festival. And there are plenty more to add to that list. For a dedicated oenophile, wine-producing regions close to Los Angeles like Paso Robles, Temecula, Santa Barbara, and the Santa Ynez Valley all provide golden opportunities for a day or weekend away.

Stellies Wines specializes in South African Stellenbosch region wines. *Credit: Stellies Wines*

Spanish

Pomegranate-marinated lamb chops from Gabi James LA. *Credit: Gabi James LA*

Given the strong Spanish influence on the history of the Los Angeles Basin, you will notice Spanish architecture and street names like Alvarado Street, Camarillo Boulevard, and Junipero Avenue everywhere. The Beverly Hills City Hall was built in a Spanish Renaissance style, historic Chapman Plaza represents Spanish Colonial Revival architecture, and the Los Altos Apartments on Wilshire Boulevard are designed in Mission Revival style. The Biltmore Los Angeles close by has its own historical significance thanks to its many architectural styles.

In addition, the list of Los Angeles Historic Cultural Monuments includes the Central Spanish Seventh-Day Adventist Church in Westlake and the Spanish-American War Memorial in Pershing Square. The memorial is the city's oldest piece of public art and also its first public monument. The park at Pershing Square is an outdoor concert and event center frequented by people of many cultures, suitable for enjoying the pleasant Los Angeles weather conditions almost year-round. Street food vendors, Cinco de Mayo celebrations, a series of Divercity Summer Concerts, and other special programming events are vying for people's attention almost every weekend. There's always something fun to do in LA.

Food And Celebrations

- Afro-Latinx Festival
- Bowery Bungalow
- Casa Cordoba
- Gabi James Los Angeles
- Gasolina Café Mercado Vino
- La Española Meats
- La Lo La Rooftop
- La Paella Tapas and Wine
- Los Angeles International Flamenco Festival
- Los Angeles Libros Festival
- Manchego
- National Hispanic Heritage Month
- Newfilmmakers Los Angeles Monthly Film Festival | InFocus: Latinx & Hispanic Cinema
- San Laurel restaurant
- Spain restaurant
- Tatel Beverly Hills
- Teleferic Barcelona
- The Serrano Experience
- Vino wine and tapas bar
- Xuntos restaurant

Organizations And Institutions

- Arcadia Spanish-American War Memorial at Arcadia Community Regional Park
- Bilingual Foundation of the Arts
- Dominguez Rancho Adobe Museum
- El Pueblo de Los Angeles Historical Monument
- Geffen Playhouse
- Heart of Samba Entertainment
- Instituto Cervantes of Los Angeles
- La Plaza de Cultura y Artes
- Latino Community Foundation
- Los Angeles Guitar Festival
- Los Angeles Metropolitan Hispanic Chambers of Commerce
- Los Angeles Public Library International Languages Department
- Reforma Los Angeles
- St. Mark's Episcopal Church
- Subsuelo music
- Sur La Table Spanish cooking classes

Food And Celebrations

- 23rd Street Café
- Abhiruchi Grill
- Apey Kade
- Asian American and Pacific Islander Heritage Month in May
- Baar Baar LA
- Baja Subs Market & Deli
- Biriyani Kabob House
- Christmas celebrations
- Diwali celebrations
- Eid and Ramadan celebrations
- Flavors of Asia grocery store
- Independence Day celebrations
- Indo Lanka Cash and Carry
- Kapoor's Akbar
- Mayura
- Pearl Island Restaurant
- Plate 50 LA restaurant
- Shor
- Sinhala Tamil New Year celebrations
- Sri Lanka Day
- Sri Lankan Delight grocery store

Organizations And Institutions

- America Sri Lanka Photographic Art Society
- Consulate General of Sri Lanka
- Dharma Vijaya Buddhist Vihara
- Hindu Temple and Cultural Center
- International Society for Krishna Consciousness
- Islamic Center of Southern California
- King Fahad Mosque
- Southern California Cricket Association
- Sri Lanka American Association of Southern California
- Sri Lanka Foundation International
- Sri Lanka Muslim Association of California
- Sri Lankarama Buddhist Temple
- The Norton Simon Museum South and Southeast Asian Painting and Sculpture Collection

Sri Lankan

There is a large population of Sri Lankans that has made the city of Los Angeles their home. A sprinkling of restaurants, grocers, and places of worship catering to the community is one indicator of where Sri Lankans may have settled but the community is represented within the San Fernando Valley in cities like Reseda and Tarzana or more toward the south, closer to Little India in Artesia. Dining venues like Apey Kade and Baja Sub Sri Lankan are two of the well-known locations where you can find traditional cuisine such as stringhoppers (steamed flour in noodle form shaped in circles), lamprais (lumped rice combined with a variety of ingredients and packed in a banana leaf), and wattalappan (coconut custard).

Several Sri Lankan-owned businesses have come and gone in the last few years so if you find recommendations online, best to research ahead before making any place your destination. While several cultural events are hosted through the year to bring the community together, the festivities are much more elaborate for the Sinhala Tamil New Year and Sri Lanka Day celebrations, sometimes featuring dance and musical performances, so watch out for when those dates are announced annually.

Sri Lankan stringhoppers can be served savory or sweet. *Credit: Ruksana Hussain*

Swedish

Established in 2010, Sockerbit has hundreds of candy options. *Credit Sockerbit*

For most Angelenos, the mention of Sweden begins and ends with the Swedish-based Ikea home-goods store in Burbank, which opened to much excitement when it started operations in the city. For those who don't have an Ikea near them, this is a mandatory shopping stop. But Los Angeles has an active Swedish community and many Scandinavian-owned businesses are based here. There are festivities throughout the year and bakeries aplenty to satisfy your sweet tooth with Swedish pastries.

For a similar experience in Culver City, you can visit Copenhagen Pastry, a Danish pastry shop. Both the Paramount Pictures studio and the Sony Pictures studio are nearby if you'd like to experience a studio tour while in LA. If in Burbank, the Warner Brothers studio tour is easily one of the top things to do. Another unique experience when it comes to studios is being an on-air audience member, a true Hollywood flex. Plan in advance using one of the many websites where you can sign up to be part of the audience on talk shows and other live entertainment such as *America's Got Talent*, *Dancing with the Stars*, and *Jimmy Kimmel Live*, among many others.

Food And Celebrations

- Ava Krō
- Berolina Bakery
- Bulle Bakery
- Clark Street Bread
- Huset shop
- ilcaffè los angeles
- Malibu Farm Restaurant and Café
- Midsummer celebrations
- National Day celebrations
- Nordic Oscars Week celebrations
- Nordic Spirit Symposium
- Open Face Food Shop
- Scandinavian Festival
- Scandinavian Film Festival
- Shoop's European Deli and Café
- Sockerbit Swedish Candy Shop
- Swedish Christmas Fair
- The Magic Nut and Candy Co.
- Valborg spring celebration
- Viking Pizza and Kabob

Organizations And Institutions

- & other stories clothing store
- Acne Studios clothing
- COS clothing
- Duxiana Furniture store
- European Languages and Movies in America
- Fjällräven North America
- H&M clothing
- Happy Socks
- Hästens Beds
- Ikea
- Los Angeles Public Library International Languages Department
- Nordic Spirit Classics Second Friday Series
- Nudie Jeans Co.
- Ragdoll clothing
- Scandinavian American Cultural and Historical Foundation
- Swedes in Los Angeles Facebook group
- Swedish American Chamber of Commerce
- Swedish Prints store
- Swedish Women's Educational Association Los Angeles Chapter
- The Consulate of Sweden in Los Angeles

Food And Celebrations

- Al Basch Chicken
- Aleppo Grill
- Ammatoli
- Arab American Heritage Month celebrations in April
- Borjstar Shawarma Shop
- Bowery Bungalow
- Easter and Christmas celebrations
- Eid and Ramadan celebrations
- Glendale Shawarma
- Independence Day celebrations
- Jewish American Heritage Month celebrations in May
- Kebab Halebi
- Kobee Factory Syrian Kitchen
- Koko's
- Mush Bakery
- Nawal
- New Arrival Supper Club
- NewFilmmakers Los Angeles Film Festival InFocus: Middle Eastern & Arab Cinema
- Sincerely Syria
- West LA International Market

Organizations And Institutions

- A Country Called Syria
- CAIR Greater Los Angeles | SoCal Muslim Empowerment
- Craft Contemporary
- Islamic Center of Hawthorne
- Islamic Center of Southern California
- Little Arabia district
- Los Angeles County Museum of Art Islamic Art Collection
- Los Angeles County Museum of Art Middle East Collection
- Los Angeles Public Library International Languages Department
- Magen David Congregation of Beverly Hills
- Masjid Al-Noor
- Mediterranean Market at Farmers Market
- Miry's List
- Younes and Soraya Nazarian Center for the Performing Arts

Syrian

A large part of the Los Angeles Syrian community comprises refugees dispersed across the city. So when Little Amal visited Los Angeles, all eyes were on the local Syrian-American community. The 12-foot-tall puppet represented a 10-year-old Syrian refugee girl. Amal means hope in Arabic and the message was one of hope in shedding light on the Syrian refugees and their stories of resilience in the face of hardship. She visited 15 countries and more than 100 cities. Toward the end of 2023 when she made it to the United States and stopped by the City of Angels, Little Amal was a champion of global human rights for refugees everywhere. Of course, moving to a new country can be challenging. Fortunately, there are nonprofits like Miry's List to help smooth the process with creative solutions such as the New Arrival Supper Club. Supper clubs are intimate dining experiences hosted in different settings intended to be a communal experience allowing for interaction between diners. Now many neighborhoods have one though not necessarily focused on refugee relations. Search online for one near you, or watch out for the next event on Miry's List.

Ammatoli's Levantine cuisine serves up decadent traditional dishes. *Credit: Ammatoli*

Maria Khani and Dania Alkhouli help dismantle stereotypes about Syria. *Credit: A Country Called Syria*

Taiwanese

Samuel Wang's Steep LA modern tearoom serves premium teas and tea-based cocktails. *Credit: Steep LA*

Los Angeles has the largest Taiwanese community in the United States. During AAPI Heritage Month in May, the Taiwanese host their own celebrations for American Heritage Week. Monterey Park—also known unofficially as Little Taipei—has the largest presence, but other areas such as Rowland Heights and Hacienda Heights have large Taiwanese communities as well. Monterey Park also hosts an annual Lunar New Year celebration and a Cherry Blossom Festival, both of which offer food, performances, art, and craft vendors to showcase Asian cultures. But the plethora of restaurants in the City of Angels ensures that you don't have to go too far to get a taste of the cuisine with dishes like noodles and oyster, meatball dumplings, and ice mango and sago. If boba tea (traditional milk tea made with tapioca balls or pearls) is your beverage of choice, then there is likely to be a tea shop nearby with a flavor you like no matter the neighborhood. Using one of the many "Best of Boba Tea Shops in Los Angeles" lists for reference is a good idea. And while you are at it, you won't want to miss out on their hearty and delicious beef noodle soup.

Pine and Crane DTLA is a casual Taiwanese restaurant in South Park. *Credit: Tanveer Badal*

Food And Celebrations

- Bafang Dumpling
- Boba Bear
- Boiling Point Hot Pot Restaurant
- Bubble U Bubble Tea Shop
- Dear Bella Creamery
- Jellyman Tea Room
- Joy on York
- Kato Omakase
- La Sinbala Restaurant
- Little Fatty
- Liu's Café
- Los Angeles Asian Pacific Film Festival
- Lunar New Year
- Mee and Greet
- Meet Fresh Dessert Shop
- Peace Lantern Festival
- Pine and Crane
- Steep LA Tea Room
- Taiwanese American Heritage Week celebrations
- Tiger Sugar Boba Desserts
- Wushiland Boba Bubble Tea Shop

Organizations And Institutions

- Asian Pacific Community Fund
- Bliss and Wisdom Los Angeles
- Evangelical Formosan Church of Alhambra
- Global Federation of Chinese Business Women Southern California
- Gu Grocery Chinese Taiwanese Family Food Project
- Hsi Lai Temple
- Los Angeles County Museum of Art South and Southeast Asian Art Collection
- Taipei Economic and Cultural Office
- Taiwan Academy Los Angeles
- Taiwan Center of Greater Los Angeles
- Taiwanese American Professionals Los Angeles chapter
- TaiwaneseAmerican.org

Food And Celebrations

- Asian American and Pacific Islander Heritage Month in May
- Ayara Thai
- Bhan Kanom Thai
- East Hollywood Farmers Market
- Emporium Thai
- Farmhouse Kitchen
- Friends and Family
- Harvard and Stone
- Holy Basil
- Jitlada Southern Thai
- Kruang Tedd
- Lacha Somtum
- Mae Malai House of Noodles
- Night & Market
- Otus Thai Kitchen & Coffee
- Palms Thai
- Radna Silom
- Same Same
- Sanamlunag Café
- Soongkran New Year Celebration
- Sri Siam Café
- Tabula Rasa
- The Silverlake House by Leela Thai
- Tuk Tuk Thai

Organizations And Institutions

- atSiam Night Market
- Kadampa Meditation Center
- Los Angeles County Library Asian Pacific Resource Center
- Los Angeles County Museum of Art South and Southeast Asian Art Collection
- Norton Simon Museum South and Southeast Asian Painting and Sculpture Collection
- Nuad Royal Spa
- Royal Thai Consulate General in Los Angeles
- Thai Association of Southern California
- Thai Community Arts and Cultural Center
- Thai Community Development Center
- Thai Town Council
- Wat Thai Buddhist Temple

Thai

Jitlada's Southern Thai cuisine has an extensive menu.
Credit: Jitlada

Los Angeles has the only officially recognized Thai Town in the country, probably because the Thai population here is the largest outside of Thailand. Hard to miss this stretch along Hollywood Boulevard—the signage is written in Thai everywhere and there are a myriad of businesses on either side of the street offering everything from Thai food and gifts to spas and groceries, among other services.

Over the years, many celebrities have lived in the Trianon Apartments located in Thai Town Los Angeles. The apartments have been designated a Historic-Cultural Monument for their architectural style resembling a French castle. Close to it is the Apsonsi Thai angel statue that serves as the Gateway to Thai Town, another historical marker for the community. Venues for viewing Thai artworks and more include the USC Pacific Asia Museum and the Over The Influence Gallery in the Arts District. Celebrity Chef Jet Tila is known for his contributions to the local Thai community and for bringing visibility to the cuisine globally since he received the first ceremonial title of culinary ambassador for Thailand presented by the Royal Thai Consulate General in Los Angeles.

Farmhouse Thai features classic and contemporary dishes.
Credit: Farmhouse Kitchen Thai Cuisine

Thai : Service, space, and spice come together at Tuk Tuk Thai on Sawtelle Boulevard. ***Credit: Hannah Khan***

Turkish

At Miry's List, the new arrival supper club welcomes new families resettling in Los Angeles. *Credit: Miry's List*

If you are in Los Angeles, you won't have to go too far to enjoy the wonders of Turkish culture. Bakeries, cafés, and other eateries serving Turkish coffee and sweet treats like baklava (filo pastry dessert), knafeh (filo dough dessert), and helva (made with flour and sugar) can be found throughout the metro area, and Long Beach hosts a Turkish Festival every June. Unfortunately, the only Turkish bath house in the city has closed permanently so the closest you can get to such an experience would be a hammam service at The Raven Spa or a Himalayan salt sauna at the LA City Spa. However, if you wish to find a similar experience, try the halotherapy or salt rooms that are common in Los Angeles. Therapeutic and relaxing, the Salt Studio, Valley Salt Cave, Crystal Salt Cave, and Halo Salt Spa each include a salt cave or some version of it for a halotherapy experience. Equally common in LA are float spas featuring sensory deprivation, but for a fully immersive sensory experience, Los Angeles always has an accessible handful of immersive exhibitions or pop-up experiences to try. Check out Yayoi Kusama's Infinity Mirrors at The Broad for starters.

Turkish coffee is great but tea has its own charm too. *Credit: Ruksana Hussain*

Food And Celebrations

Agora World Market

Alchemist Cafe & Restaurant

Baklava Factory

Bavel

Bibi's Bakery

Bowery Bungalow

Café Istanbul

California Turkish Festival Long Beach

Dolan's Uyghur Cuisine

Doner G

Doner Turco

Eid and Ramadan celebrations

Galata Halal Eatery

JeJe Mediterranean Grill

Kismet

Levant Mediterranean Restaurant

Muma Kitchen

Nuka Café

Sevan Garden Kebab House

South East European Film Festival

Spitz Los Feliz

Sumac Modern Street Food

West LA International Market

Yalla Truck

Organizations And Institutions

Anatolia Cultural Centers

Association of Turkish Americans of Southern California

Craft Contemporary

Fowler Museum

Hive Gallery and Studios

Islamic Center of Southern California

Los Angeles County Museum Art of the Middle East Collection

Los Angeles Turkish American Association

Miry's List

UCLA Sephardic Archive Initiative

University of California Los Angeles Herb Alpert School of Music Turkey Ensemble

USC Fisher Museum of Art

Food And Celebrations

Annual Pysanka Festival

Babushka Deli

Celebration of Hannukah: Festival of Lights in December

Christmas celebrations

EuroAsia Restaurant

European Deli Market

Kashtan Restaurant and Deli

Mechta International Deli

Mom, Please Ukrainian Food

Oliv'e Food Market

Otto's European and Hungarian Import Store & Deli

Pacific Coast Food

South East European Film Festival

Strada Eateria and Bar

Sweets A LA-Cluj

Tashkent Produce

Traktir

Ukrainefest

Ukrainian Independence Day celebrations

West LA International Market

World Refugee Day

Organizations And Institutions

'i am u are' Ukrainian Creators Fair & Exhibition

Chervona Kalyna Dance Ensemble

Kyiv to LA

Los Angeles County Museum of Art European Painting and Sculpture Collection

Los Angeles Public Library International Languages Department

Mosaic Orchestra

Nativity of the Blessed Virgin Mary Ukrainian Catholic Church

Pro-Cathedral of Saint Vladimir (Ukrainian Orthodox)

Ukrainian Art Center

Ukrainian Culture Center

Ukraine United Association

Wende Museum

Ukrainian

The Ukrainian Culture Center in Los Angeles is a good place to start with your experience of Eastern European culture in the city. There are events hosted here throughout the year including music performances by the Ukrainian National Choir of California and dance performances by Chervona Kalyna LA Ukrainian Dance Ensemble, community celebrations for Christmas, fundraisers supporting rehabilitation efforts in Ukraine since the Russian invasion in 2022, and other ways for the community to interact. The Culture Center is at the historic Jensen Theatre building on Melrose Avenue, which has many other points of interest if you decide to wander along that busy street. There are several smaller performance venues like the Skiptown Playhouse, Blackout Cinema, Yard Theatre, and Cat's Crawl where you can watch a show. Or you may wish to visit the Los Angeles Museum of Love. Melrose Avenue is famed for its many Insta-walls, providing artsy backgrounds for social media-worthy selfies and photographic mementos. Notable among these are the Paul Smith Pink Wall (which has become a tourist attraction with its own Instagram account featuring the blank pink wall), Mural Alley, and Art Wall. Angel wings mural walls can also be seen in multiple locations.

Mom, Please Ukrainian Food's cottage cheese pancakes.
Credit: Mom, Please Ukrainian Food

Uzbek

Lazzat Grill's Uzbek dishes include kurutob with meat. *Credit Ruksana Hussain*

A few thousand Uzbeks live in Los Angeles. They do not yet have a cultural center as such but the community is sufficiently represented by a handful of restaurants that cater specifically to the needs of the Uzbek Angelenos and the members of neighboring countries. Notable among those restaurants is Lazzat Grill, which has a food truck and a restaurant location as well. The community also celebrates Navroz in the spring, as do many communities with some Persian influence.

Los Angeles has its fair share of spring events although not all are culturally significant. There's the Los Angeles Spring Fair, Spring Classic Horse Show, The Other Art Faire, Renaissance Pleasure Faire, and the Beverly Hills Art Show, all within the March-through-May spring season. Spring is also the perfect time to find farmers' markets across the city where fresh spring produce makes its annual appearance. Some of the best (which may or may not have a little petting-zoo opportunity going on when you visit) are in Santa Monica, Hollywood, Studio City, Altadena, Malibu, and Beverly Hills. Some markets have a band playing that day so you even get a little free concert experience during your visit.

Food And Celebrations

- Asian American and Pacific Islander Heritage Month in May
- Eid and Ramadan celebrations
- EuroAsia Restaurant
- Halal Kitchen Café
- Independence Day celebration in September
- Lazzat Grill
- Los Angeles Asian Film Festival
- Mante House
- Melad Bakery Restaurant and Catering
- Naan Daagh Kabob Daagh restaurant
- Navat Shawarma and Central Asian Food Truck
- Navruz spring celebrations
- New Arrivals Supper Club
- Remembrance Day in May
- Saffron Food Mart
- Shor
- Skewers Halal

Organizations And Institutions

- Islamic Center of Southern California
- King Fahad Mosque
- Masjid Bilal Islamic Center
- Miry's List
- Southern California Halal Foodies Instagram
- The Norton Simon Museum South and Southeast Asian Painting and Sculpture Collection
- University of California Los Angeles Asia Pacific Center Program on Central Asia
- University of Southern California Los Angeles Department of Slavic, East European and Eurasian Languages and Cultures
- West LA International Market

Food And Celebrations

- African Obichi Food Store
- Afro-Latinx Festival
- Amara Café
- Bachata and Salsa Dance Festival
- Café Bolivar
- Cariaco Bodega
- Chainsaw LA
- Chamo Venezuelan Cuisine
- Dat Moi Market
- Día de los Difuntos
- Día de Todos los Santos
- Dog.R Venezuelan Hot Dogs
- Independence celebrations in July
- La Casa de las Parilladas
- La Fonda Antioqueña
- La Maria
- National Hispanic Heritage Month
- Nova Bakery
- Obra Bakery
- Sus Arepas
- The Arepa Stand
- Tito's Market
- Tropic Ice Dessert Shop
- Vivi's Gourmet Cuisine
- WezzArepas

Organizations And Institutions

- Avenue 50 Studio
- Bermudez Projects
- Bilingual Foundation of the Arts
- Craft in America Center
- Iglesia Evangelica Latina
- International Society of Black Latinos
- La Diosa
- La Galeria Rebelde
- La Placita Church
- La Plaza de Cultura y Artes
- Latino Outdoors
- Latino Theater Company
- Little Venezuela Hollywood
- Museum of Latin American Art
- Quitanda Family Market
- Salsa and Bachata Los Angeles Facebook group
- The Granada
- The Broad
- The Mistake Room

Venezuelan

Los Angeles has the largest Venezuelan community in the state. Most Angelenos know of Gustavo Dudamel, the Venezuelan-born music director of the LA Philharmonic. In fact, LA Phil is considered one of the best orchestras in the world, playing at the downtown Walt Disney Hall (designed by Frank Gehry) or in the Hollywood Bowl during the summer months. LA Phil's Youth Orchestra (YOLA) music education program is an adaptation of Venezuela's El Sistema music education program. Other venues where you can enjoy live musical performances include El Rey Theatre, Staples Center, Hollywood Palladium, The Novo, and Troubadour. The Music Center's Dance DTLA, Sunday Sessions at Gloria Molina Grand Park, KCRW Summer Nights, Summer Music at the Original Farmers Market Plaza, and Off The 405 at the Getty Center are all outdoor musical events. Watch for performances by Los Angeles-based Venezuelan band Venezuela Oye Mi Gaita or Venezuela OMG specializing in Venezuelan folk music. Oye Mi Gaita translates to listen to my gaita and gaita is a style of music from the western parts of the country dating to the 1950s. Another loved musical style is joropo—if you find a performance you can attend, don't miss it!

The Sus Arepas food truck brings South American cuisine to LA neighborhoods. *Credit: Sus Arepas*

Sus Arepas menu includes options like original, rumbera, and reina. *Credit: Sus Arepas*

Vietnamese

Nam's Vietnamese Coffee Shop has three distinct Vietnamese coffee including a signature coffee from the Highlands of Vietnam. *Credit: NamCoffee*

Though Little Saigon is in Orange County, the Vietnamese American community is dispersed across Los Angeles, with large populations in Rosemead, the San Gabriel Valley, and other areas. Multiple Lunar New Year or Tet celebrations are hosted by the community, during which you can score a festive Vietnamese meal at several area restaurants. Asian American and Pacific Islander Month festivities are also a great way to immerse yourself in local Vietnamese culture. Meanwhile, the Thiên Ân and Lạc Hồng Performing Arts groups celebrate with music and dance performances at multiple venues and events during citywide celebrations. In any season, there are many options when it comes to finding the perfect dining spot for pho (rice noodle soup), banh mi (sandwich with meat and other fillings), and other favorites. For a taste of Vietnamese/French cuisine with California ingredients, Crustacean Beverly Hills beckons. Owners Elizabeth An and Chef Helene An have nurtured a gastronomic treasure trove. Chef Helene, well-known in Los Angeles culinary circles, was inducted into the California Hall of Fame in 2024 for her impact on the culinary world. When dining here, recommended dishes from the menu are Tuna Cigars, Ube soufflé pancakes, and Cacio e Pepe ramen.

Crustacean's Ube Souffle Pancakes is a popular dish. *Credit: Crustacean Beverly Hills*

Food And Celebrations

Aquarium of the Pacific Southeast Asia Day festival

Asia Supermarket

Asian American and Pacific Islander Heritage Month in May

Au Lac

Be U Kitchen

Cassia restaurant

Crustacean Beverly Hills

Gingergrass

It's Pho

Kien Giang Bakery

Little Sister

Lokal Sandwich Shop + Burger Bar

Los Angeles Asian Pacific Film Festival

Los Angeles Public Library Asian Pacific American Heritage Month

Mama Hong's Vietnamese Kitchen

Mee and Greet

My Lai Kitchen

Nam Coffee

Nong La Café

Pho Gyu Noodle House

Pho Saigon Pearl

Phorage

The Sister's Café

Viet Film Fest

Organizations And Institutions

2T Media and Music

Arcadia Vietnam War Monument at Arcadia Community Regional Park

Los Angeles County Library Asian Pacific Resource Center

Los Angeles County Museum of Art South and Southeast Asian Art Collection

Los Angeles Public Library International Languages Department

The Norton Simon Museum South and Southeast Asian Painting and Sculpture Collection

Thien Hau Temple

USC Pacific Asia Museum

Vietnamese American Arts and Letters Association

Vietnamese American Chamber of Commerce

West Los Angeles Buddhist Temple

Grandmaster Recorders interior.
Credit: Jennifer Johnson

Index